Beyond the Spectrum: A Guide to Parenting Adolescents With Autism

Navigating Challenges, Cultivating Strengths, and Fostering Independence

Richard Bass

2 FREE Bonuses!

Receive a FREE <u>Planner for Kids</u> and a copy of the <u>Positive Discipline Playbook</u> by scanning below!

Table of Contents

Introduction

I might hit developmental and societal milestones in a different order than my peers, but I am able to accomplish these small victories on my own time.
–Haley Moss

Those teenage years between 13 and 18 are a rollercoaster! And that's before considering the impact of living with a cognitive disability. Research shows that teenagers with autism are at a higher risk of developing anxiety and depression due to the amount of challenges they may face at school and among their peer group (Raising Children Network, 2023).

The idea of being "different" from others may not have been an issue for your child when they were in preschool or middle school. Sure, they picked up on the fact that learning and memorizing information didn't come easy for them, or that they had trouble interpreting social cues. But that didn't stop them from trying to integrate into the classroom and social environments.

As a teenager, being different from others may be something that eats away at your child's self-esteem and causes them to have difficult relationships with you, their siblings, school teachers, and classmates. The increasing expectations at home and at school, as well as the pressure to fit in with the crowd, can make surviving these adolescent years feel painful.

Acting out and breaking rules are common behaviors at this stage of life for any teen. However, for a young person who is simultaneously managing autism symptoms while also attempting to find their place in the world, these difficult behaviors can be more intense and frequent.

Steve Jobs, who was rumored to be on the spectrum, had similar challenges during high school. His school teachers would have called him a "difficult child" because of the constant power struggles he entered with them. In an interview, Jobs once admitted that he would stir up trouble in class because he was bored. His fascination was with computer parts and electronics, not with being asked to "memorize stupid stuff" (Stevenson, 2021). Like any other different child, he was bullied a lot and often misunderstood as being rebellious, when in reality he simply needed to be challenged.

His parents were more compassionate than his school teachers, that's for sure. They worked with Jobs to create a healthy and productive environment. This meant having to change schools a few times and expose their child to side interests and hobbies. He joined the Explorer's Club at Hewlett-Packard, where engineers at the company would engage with a group of students and discuss what they were working on. The Explorer's Club was where Jobs saw the first computer in-person and was introduced to his mentor Larry Lang, who would play an instrumental role in his life.

There's no doubt that Steve Jobs and other teenagers living with autism are different. However, depending on who you ask, their differences can be a strength rather than a weakness. The cumbersome task of parents is to sing a different tune from the world and be their children's biggest cheerleaders. Instead of attempting to change their children, forcing them to do what other teenagers their age are doing, parents can adjust their children's home and social environments to offer more support and positive reinforcement.

Beyond the Spectrum will teach parents various skills and approaches to parenting teenagers with autism to help them gain more confidence disciplining their children on the spectrum, while also being responsive to their needs for space, respect, and independence. What makes this book different from normal teenage self-help books are the strategies presented, which are specific to the needs and sensitivities of teenagers with autism.

Adolescence is a bumpy road for normal teens, but the pressure and demands are higher for neurodivergent teens, who may need extra support at home and at school managing physical, behavioral, and social changes. Parents can make the transition from adolescence to adulthood more enjoyable and comfortable for their children by playing a supportive role.

Since this book encourages healthy parent-child relationships, you will find exercises for parents *and teenagers* at the end of each chapter!

Chapter 1:

The Transition From

Adolescence to Adulthood

*Adolescence is like having only enough light to see the step directly in front of you. —*Sarah Addison Allen

The Troubled Teen Who Revolutionized the World of Physics

Did you know the Father of Modern Physics, Albert Einstein, was labeled a "troubled teen" during his adolescent years? This was due to his academic challenges and run-ins with authority at school. Some researchers who investigated Einstein's childhood years believe that he displayed signs of mild autism or Asperger's Syndrome, while others disagree (Eagle Ranch Academy, 2015).

Below are some of the cognitive and behavioral struggles he experienced as a teenager:

- Einstein experienced slow development as a child, which caused delays with speech and learning.

- He didn't take interest in many subjects, except physics and mathematics. Einstein was fascinated by things that other children didn't notice or care about, such as the concepts of space and time.

- As a teenager, Einstein frequently engaged in power struggles with school teachers. One of his headmasters told him that he wouldn't amount to anything, while another expelled him from the school.

Despite his difficulty at school, Einstein never lost his passion for physics and mathematics. After graduating from college, he looked for jobs within academia and in the meantime worked on his doctoral dissertation. He struggled to find an academic job, perhaps because he didn't look like your typical professor. His doctoral dissertation was also rejected several times.

Eventually, Einstein settled for a job at a Swiss patent office, working six days a week. Up until then, his future seemed hopeless to many people. But what they didn't know was that he was spending all of his free time working diligently on five groundbreaking scientific papers. The first paper was submitted for his doctorate, and he passed with flying colors. The remaining four papers would completely transform his career and change how the world understood the universe. The topics of these papers were

- **the Brownian movement**: the discovery of microscopic molecules moving in a zigzag motion when suspended in liquids or gasses;

- **the quantum theory of light**: the discovery that light travels in separate bundles of energy, known as *photons* or *quanta*, which are made up of both waves and particles;

- **the theory of special relativity**: the discovery that the speed of light is a limit that other material objects can approach but not reach; and

- **the relationship between mass and energy**: Einstein found a connection between mass and energy, outlined in his famous scientific equation: $E = mc^2$. He discovered that mass and energy represent the same physical entity and can be converted into each other.

Society often puts pressure on adolescence to grow up a certain way, achieve certain grades at school, and relate to their peers in the same fashion. Teens who are on the spectrum—or live with other mental impairments—can sometimes feel rejected by their peers for displaying uncommon traits. However, what Albert Einstein proved is that the so-called troubled teen can be a closet genius who simply needs to be placed in the right environment to flourish.

Every teen with autism can have their turnaround moment, but only when they are given an opportunity to reveal their strengths and plenty of positive reinforcement to help them bounce back from developmental setbacks!

What Is Adolescence?

Adolescence is a transitory period between childhood and adulthood. It occurs between the ages of 13 and 18. During this time, children become teenagers and prepare for life as young adults.

When you as a parent understand that this is a transitory period, you are able to make sense of the physical, mental, emotional, and behavioral changes in your child. The theme of change is central during adolescence, as every aspect of your child's life is transformed.

Take a moment and consider your openness or reluctance to change. Think about the last time you went through a life transition, such as moving homes or changing jobs. Try to imagine how you felt during the highs and lows of the transition.

Adolescence is one of the first major transitions that your child will experience before entering adulthood and facing more complex transitions. During this six-year period, they will change right before your eyes. They can either change for the worse or become a better version of themselves, depending on how prepared they are to manage the highs and lows of adolescence.

Put yourself in their shoes. What might they be feeling right now? The major recurring emotion your child may feel is fear. For instance, they might fear the unknown, going to college, not being able to make it through high school, and so on.

When human beings—regardless of their age or gender—are fearful, their stress response is activated, and how they perceive reality shifts. Due to the fear of the unknown, for example, your child may have a very negative perception of the future. They might believe that there is nothing to look forward to because the world is rapidly changing for the worse.

Living with autism creates fears of its own, such as the fear of being socially accepted by others, building healthy relationships (and finding a soulmate), and being able to build a successful career and manage the demands of adulthood.

There are five major areas of your child's life that will undergo change. It is important for you to be mindful of the challenges your child may face in each area and do your best to support them. The following subsections outline each area and examples of the changes your child may experience. Note that these are changes that affect most teenagers, including (but not specifically) teens with autism.

Physical Changes

One of the notable changes you will see in your child during adolescence is a growth spurt. Within a short period of time, their body weight, height, and physical appearance will transform. The series of physical changes that occur is known as puberty.

For some teens, puberty can start before they reach 13 years old, and for others, it may start well within their adolescent years. What determines the exact time puberty starts for your child is the release of certain hormones in their body. This surge of hormones is responsible for the rapid growth within a short time period.

Examples what can happen during a growth spurt for girls are

- developing breasts

- The start of menstruation

- facial acne

- mood swings

- noticeable hair on different body parts

Examples of what can happen during a growth spurt for boys are

- voice changes

- muscle growth

- facial acne

- mood swings

- wet dreams

- growth of reproductive organs

Since these physical changes don't happen at the same time for every teenager, it's possible for your child to feel self-conscious about their experience with puberty. For example, your son's voice may not have cracked by the time they turn 16, or your daughter may have severe facial acne that makes her feel unattractive. The added stress of standing out from everybody can be a real cause for concern in their life and something that preoccupies their mind.

Cognitive Changes

During adolescence, there are also some mental developments that happen. Once again, these changes may not hit teenagers at the same time or in the same way. One of the most noticeable mental shifts you will witness in your child is their ability to move away from concrete, narrow thinking to abstract, lateral thinking.

A typical example of this is noticing your child contemplating their identity beyond the superficial elements like their name, age, gender, and likes/dislikes. The question of "Who am I?" lingers at the back of their mind as they interact with friends and family and experience more opportunities to express themselves or set boundaries.

Due to the broadening of their mind, your child may even start to question rules, routines, and processes that they previously didn't have a problem with. Instead of blindly following the rules, they could be curious about the value or intention behind them. Be prepared for your child to frequently ask "why?" whenever they are given an instruction. At face value, this may look like a pushback, but it's their way of making sense of principles.

Scientists have discovered that the prefrontal cortex takes the longest to develop in adolescents. This is the front region of the brain that is responsible for emotional regulation, pattern recognition, impulse control, and planning and coordination. It is therefore common to find teenagers who have the capacity to think laterally and question ideas, but not enough bandwidth to reflect deeply on thoughts and behaviors and make good judgment calls.

Other issues that this may cause include egocentric behavior, increased risk-taking without consideration of the consequences, emotional outbursts, and unexplained mood swings. You can help your child engage their prefrontal cortex by helping them understand cause and effect, teaching them how to empathize with others, and asking questions to help them challenge their own ideas.

Emotional Changes

One of the most difficult changes for teenagers to manage are their unstable emotions. Due to a surge of hormones flowing in their bodies, teens are more likely to react in impulsive, irrational, and overly emotional ways.

Some of the common experiences that both teenage girls and boys will have include

- frequent mood swings

- unpredictable emotional outbursts

- feeling easily overwhelmed by stressful events

- sensitivity to criticism

- indecisiveness

- feeling self-conscious about their bodies

- negative self-talk/negative thinking

What makes adolescence particularly challenging is that teens have only a few years to prepare for adulthood. As you can imagine, or recall from your own past, the pressure to know your place in the world can create a lot of stress and emotional distress.

Most teenagers don't know what to do when their stress levels rise and life starts to feel heavy. Thus, they turn to the best coping mechanisms they can find, which are usually technology, spending more time with friends, or self-isolating. It is also common for parents to have frequent arguments with their children during the early years of adolescence, when the transition begins.

Social Changes

One of the important themes for teenagers during adolescence is identity. This theme isn't a big deal when children are young, but as soon as they reach the stage of questioning, they are more curious about forming an identity.

By nature, human beings are social creatures. We feel more fulfilled and confident when we are part of a group or have connections with different people. Peer groups are essential for helping teenagers discover who they are and where they fit in the world. Through building friendships, they are able to develop a healthy self-esteem and learn crucial interpersonal skills.

If your child doesn't have a lot of friends when they reach adolescence, they may start to yearn for connection. On an instinctive level, they feel a part of their identity missing without having peers to validate who they are. Therefore, to form a solid sense of self, they need access to welcoming circles of friends who can cheer them on, offer emotional support, and help your child find their voice.

It isn't expected for teenagers to have perfect social skills or maintain all of their friendships. What's important is getting enough practice in sharing their thoughts and feelings with others and receiving positive feedback. Online texting and socializing can to some degree help teens make connections; however, when the only source of connection they get is through social media or online gaming, they are vulnerable to developing loneliness, social anxiety, and depression.

Moral Changes

Another type of change your teenager may go through is rethinking and reorganizing their belief systems. Up until this point in their life, they relied on the wisdom taught by you, elderly family members, school teachers, and the community.

Your child happily adopted your own personal views about life, health, career, politics, and religion. But now that they're beginning to think more broadly about life, they are starting to entertain ideas of their own.

Moral changes start by asking questions and seeking clarity about widely accepted ideas and beliefs. If your child doesn't see the logic or find the value in a certain idea or belief, they will challenge it. To some extent, external influence from friends can cause your child to question the status quo at home, school, and society at large. However, new beliefs are formed based on their own understanding and conviction about what is acceptable and unacceptable.

The tendency of most parents is to discourage open conversations, particularly around sensitive topics, out of fear of exposing their children to new ideas and perspectives. The reason why this approach doesn't work is because we live in a digital world where information is accessible outside of the home.

If you don't jump at the opportunity to educate your child on different ways of life, they will find an unqualified clout chaser on the internet who distorts their understanding of social, political, gender, and religious beliefs.

These five areas of your child's life will experience the most transformation during adolescence. The process of change can be uncomfortable for the entire family, since everybody will need to learn how to accommodate your teen during this transition.

Furthermore, living with autism makes these five areas of change that much more stressful for your child. To help them manage symptoms related to autism, consider seeking a professional medical diagnosis and treatment.

Raising a Child With Autism: From Teen to Young Adult

You have seen your child go through the toddler, preschool, and preteen stages of development while living with autism spectrum disorder (ASD). Many of the challenges you have experienced before were centered around finding the perfect routine and rituals, helping your child manage transitions from one task to another, and learning about your child's unique sensory sensitivities.

Now that they are a teenager and preparing for life as an adult, you will notice your child displaying new kinds of ASD-related symptoms. This isn't due to their disorder becoming progressively worse, but rather a result of growing up and having to deal with the challenges and responsibilities that come with adolescence.

Here are common signs of ASD in teenage girls and boys.

Difficulty Managing the Process of Puberty

Most teenagers have a difficult time adjusting to the changes that come with puberty. However, teens on the spectrum may need extra support, reminders, and clear instructions on what positive habits to practice. For instance, you may need to remind your child to shower once a day or wear deodorant. They may not be cognizant of (or always remember to follow) social cues and accepted social behaviors around manners, grooming, hygiene, and so on.

Seizures and Epilepsy

If your child is prone to having seizures or epileptic fits, they could experience them more frequently during adolescence. This has to do with the hormonal changes in their brain, which can create unusual electrical discharges. Of course, not all children on the spectrum will have seizures. If you are concerned about your child's probability of having seizures, speak to a medical doctor and get their expert opinion.

Getting in Trouble or Called In at School

Teenagers with ASD are not intentionally troublesome students. However, due to their inability to pick up on social cues, practice good communication skills, and find positive ways to self-regulate, they can sometimes get in trouble for saying or doing inappropriate things at school.

For example, your child's school teacher may yell at them for getting distracted easily in class, making jokes and disturbing other students, or blurting out something inappropriate. The more strict and regimented the school environment, the more frustrated and overwhelmed your child may feel, which would lead to them acting in inappropriate ways.

Poor Social Skills

It's common for teenagers with ASD to exhibit inappropriate social behaviors. For example, they might laugh at something serious, cross physical boundaries, play aggressively, or show a lack of empathy. Moreover, they might struggle to initiate interactions with others, maintain eye contact, or correctly interpret non-verbal cues.

The lack of tact, reciprocation, and effective social skills can make it hard for your child to build or maintain friendships. In many cases, they may feel misunderstood by others and treated unfairly. Poor social skills can also make your child vulnerable to being bullied at school, looked on unfavorably by teachers, or turned down at job interviews. Facing this much social rejection can negatively impact their sense of self-worth and make it harder to step outside of their comfort zone.

Vulnerability to Mood Disorders

One of the common feelings your child may have is being different from other people. This is a gnawing feeling that plays back in their mind, particularly when they are invalidated by others. On top of this, adolescence can be an overwhelming roller-coaster ride of hormones, which makes your child feel a lack of control over their thoughts and behaviors.

Research has shown that teenagers with ASD are at a higher risk of developing mood disorders, such as anxiety or depression, as a result of the stress they are exposed to during adolescence. One study found that as much as 39% of young people diagnosed with ASD were also diagnosed with an anxiety disorder (Wendt, 2022).

It's worth mentioning that the symptoms of ASD in teenage girls and boys may look different. This has to do with the fact that girls with ASD tend to practice a behavior known as masking, where they camouflage their symptoms and appear to have no signs of autism. They internalize the frustrations that a boy with ASD would express openly and make it seem as though they are coping.

The downside of masking is that young girls are rarely diagnosed with ASD and therefore cannot receive the medical support they need. Furthermore, they are more likely to develop unhealthy coping mechanisms, such as perfectionist thinking, to manage their hidden ASD symptoms.

If you are raising a teenage girl on the spectrum (or whom you suspect to be on the spectrum), you may need to lean in more often and check on how they are doing and what you could possibly assist them with. If they are not willing to speak openly about their challenges, consider purchasing teen-friendly cognitive behavioral therapy (CBT) and dialectical behavioral therapy (DBT) workbooks for them to work on at their own time and pace (these workbooks are also great for teenage boys with autism).

Exercise for Parents: Three Steps to Proactively Respond to Your Teen's Misbehaviors

Your child is at the stage where they are exploring the world and figuring out what's what. At some point, they will display behavior that you aren't happy with. For example, they may start to argue with their siblings more, refuse to do their chores, or say hurtful words whenever they are upset.

Instead of letting them have a free pass, waiting for the behavior to escalate before you intervene, you can take action immediately and nip it in the bud. How do you do this? By following the three steps mentioned below.

Step One: Choose a Troublesome Behavior to Focus On

Identify a single behavior that you dislike. Keep the focus on one behavior, rather than a series of small behaviors, to avoid overwhelming yourself and your child.

Example: Raising voice whenever they are given instructions to complete chores.

Step Two: Identify What Triggers the Troublesome Behavior and How It Meets Your Child's Needs

The next step is to document how the behavior usually comes about. For instance, where are you? When does it happen? And what occurs immediately before and after the behavior?

Additionally, think about how the behavior meets a certain unspoken need that your child may be feeling at the moment. Place yourself in their shoes and consider what benefit they get from it.

Example: Raising voice whenever they are given instructions to complete chores.

Where: At home

When: Each time I remind them to complete their chores.

What happens immediately before behavior: I find them watching TV, playing video games, or doing a task that involves play.

What happens immediately after the behavior: We have an argument and I walk away without getting confirmation about whether they will complete the chores or not.

It usually takes longer to identify your child's unspoken need because it requires you to step out of your own perspective and consider what they might be thinking or feeling.

From the example above, you may find that what your child really needs is respect. They raise their voice because they feel that the constant reminders are demeaning and signal a lack of trust in them. The defensive behavior is their way of standing up for themselves and showing independence, something which they may not feel you are giving them.

There could be other unspoken needs that you find, which explain—but do not justify—your child's misbehavior. Continue exploring until you gain a deeper understanding of the various ways they may be feeling.

Step Three: Make Changes to Your Own Behavior

When your child misbehaves, you might expect them to do the work of changing their behaviors. However, the first person to commit to modeling change should be you! In response to the changes in your approach, your child will adjust their approach too.

Now that you understand your child's unspoken need, think of adjustments you can make to your own behavior that can make them feel seen and accepted. For example, if reminding your child to do their chores makes them feel disrespected, perhaps you can place a visual reminder somewhere open and public (i.e., writing their chores on a kitchen chalkboard) and allow them to manage their time and decide when to complete them.

If the time to perform their chores arrives and passes without them completing it, you can simply place a cross next to their name on the chalkboard and write down the reason. All of this action is non-verbal and non-confrontational, which allows your child to make their own choices and live with the consequences of their actions. Whenever your child asks for a privilege, you can refer them to the chalkboard and kindly request for them to increase the number of ticks next to each chore instead of crosses before you can grant their privilege.

As you can see, you can positively influence your child's behaviors by changing your own. You don't need to wait until things get so bad that it is difficult to correct their behaviors. Be proactive about bringing about the change you desire in your child by taking action immediately.

Exercise for Teens: Create Your Dream Life Vision Board

Whenever we think of adolescence, we tend to get bogged down by the extreme lows and forget about the exciting opportunities that come with this transition!

Being a teenager is about preparing to become the adult you choose to be. During this short six-year period, you will learn new things about yourself and start planning for the adult life of your dreams.

One of the ways to cope with the stress and anxiety that comes with being a teen is to spend time envisioning a positive future. Daydreaming in your free time can be a great way to relax your mind and enhance positive moods.

A productive form of daydreaming is creating a vision board. A vision board is a collage of picture cutouts that represent your short-term and long-term goals on a cardboard piece of paper.

The pictures are supposed to be motivational, showing you glimpses of your ideal health status, career status, social status, financial status, relationship status, and more!

The reason why the vision board is created on paper is so that you have a visual reminder everyday about what you are working toward and why it's so important for you to keep going, even when home and school life get overwhelming.

You will need the following materials to get started:

1. Large piece of A1 or A2 cardboard paper

2. Arts and crafts supplies for decoration

3. Scissors to cut pictures

4. Glue to stick the pictures on the cardboard

5. Magazines or photos from the internet

You don't need to create your vision board in one sitting. Perhaps you can start it today and add one or two pictures on a daily or weekly basis. The aim is to think deeply about your dream life and find the best pictures that capture it. Plus, this process is supposed to be fun and stress-free, so enjoy every step of creating your board!

Chapter 2:

Your Child Will Change, but

That's Part of Growth

If your life is a blank page, that only means you have room to write your story. You have the power to tell that story the way you want to. –Thea
Harrison

Why Do Teenagers Pull Away?

If you were previously very close to your child, you will notice that they prefer spending more time alone or with their friends during early adolescence. They may not require as much closeness or quality time as they did before, which could make you wonder if there's something you are doing wrong.

The truth is that it's normal for your child to pull away at this stage of their life. Since this stage is about transitioning from childhood to adulthood, your child will experience a biological need to self-actualize.

Self-actualization is the fifth and final need on Maslow's hierarchy. It can be described as "the need or motivation to realize your full potential." In order for your child to feel as though they have reached their full potential, they need to spend a lot of time contemplating who they are, what they desire out of life, and how to relate with the world.

Unfortunately, parents and family members are rarely invited on this self-actualization journey because there must be enough space or separation created for your child to *individuate*, or become their own person. It wouldn't be possible for them to realize who they are and what they want while still being dependent on you as their parents.

Pulling away shouldn't be seen as a sign of rejection from your child, but rather a rite of passage that every young person needs to go through before becoming an independent adult. The best thing you can do during this time is to provide your child with the space they need, but also reassure them that you're available to chat whenever they need a friend or someone to listen.

What to Do When Your Child Pulls Away

The worst thing you can do when your child pulls away is to make them feel guilty for doing so. Their intention for demanding space isn't to punish you or shut you out of their life, but instead to build a separate identity from you and the family and gain a level of independence.

The good news is that there are ways to show your child that you are proud of their big decision to self-actualize and are within reach whenever they need your support. Below is a list of appropriate ways to respond whenever your teenager pulls away:

1. **Don't make it about you**: The first and possibly most important tip is to avoid making their decision to pull away from you. Challenge negative assumptions that make you feel like your child is trying to hurt you. Moreover, avoid the temptation to compare how you behaved as a teenager to how your child is behaving right now. For instance, you may have had a very close relationship with your parents throughout adolescence and never pulled away. However, that doesn't mean that your child's experience of adolescence will be the same.

2. **Show respect for their decision**: It's one thing to tell your child that you respect their decision to spend time alone, but it's another thing to display behaviors that convey respect. For example, if your child refuses to discuss a certain matter, don't push them to. Accept their wishes and don't bring up the matter again. Or, if your child spends a lot of time in their room, avoid disturbing or spying on them. If you need something,

you can knock on their door and ask for permission to enter, or send them a text with your request. The point is to accommodate their need for distance, rather than showing resistance.

3. **Continue to be emotionally available**: When your child pulls away, you shouldn't pull away either. Continue to remain present and connected to them and what is happening in their life. Of course, you may not spend as much quality time together as you did before, but in those random moments when your child decides to open up and let their guard down, show your affection and support for them. You should also continue to express kindness and offer praise, even when you don't get the feedback you are looking for. These small efforts of making a connection help your child feel safe turning inward and being a little self-focused for a while knowing that your relationship isn't jeopardized by the transition they are going through.

4. **Help your child build a support system outside of you**: As a parent, you want to know that your child has good role models to turn to when they are unwilling to come to you. It is important to help your child identify other trustworthy and responsible adults who they can seek advice from. These adults could be aunts and uncles, responsible cousins who are young adults, friends of the family, or the school counselor or sports coach. Encourage your child to maintain relationships with these individuals and reach out whenever they need help.

5. **Treat them like adults**: Every teenager will agree that the most frustrating thing their parents can do is treat them like a child. They expect to be shown the same respect and dignity that one would show an adult. While it's true that a 16-year-old and a 26-year-old are miles apart when it comes to maturity, teenagers still want to feel like they are trusted to lead their own lives. Treating your child like an adult simply means respecting their boundaries and allowing them to make their own choices. But the only way you can treat your child like an adult is if they act like one. Have an open discussion with your child about what it means to be an adult and the responsibility that comes with being given more power and control. Make a pact that you will treat them like an adult when they show you that they can act like an adult (i.e., honor their responsibilities).

Are You Guilty of Overparenting?

Parents of teenagers with autism have the tendency to become overbearing and controlling. It isn't due to not trusting their children, but rather not trusting the world or people that their children interact with.

Perhaps when their children were little, they went through difficult moments where their children got sick, hurt, or landed in trouble because of someone's negligence. Now that their children are teenagers and have access to more information, technology, and different types of people, they feel compelled to keep them close and limit the risk of encountering danger.

Take a moment to reflect on your relationship with your child. Do you resonate with the experiences of overbearing and controlling mothers? Have you lived through horrific moments that made you fearful of spending too much time away from your child? Do you have trust issues that spill over into your parent-child relationship?

In psychology, there is a term that describes this type of behavior exhibited by parents. It is called *overparenting*. Simply put, overparenting is doing more than what is required of you as a parent. It is characterized by being too needy and involved in your child's life. When they were younger and depended on you for survival needs, this type of behavior may have been harmless. However, when your child enters adolescence and seeks independence, overparenting can set them back and sabotage their chances of becoming their own person.

Overparenting is very common in parents raising children with autism. This has to do with the number of challenges and sensitivities children with autism face. It is natural for mothers to want to reduce potential for harm and create a stress-free environment for their children. However, at a certain stage, they must step back and allow their children to contend with life and develop the necessary skills required to be a confident and successful adult.

ASD comes with many dos and don'ts, which parents are taught when their children are still young. Complying with these boundaries causes children with ASD to live in a warm and safe bubble. As children get older, it is the role of parents to teach them how to survive outside of this warm and safe bubble without being overwhelmed. This means teaching them skills like how to manage triggers, overstimulation, meltdowns, unpredictable routines, and different social contexts.

Overparenting rejects this notion altogether and insists on keeping children hidden inside the bubble. While this might make both parents and children happy in the moment, it can backfire in the long run when children grow up to be needy, immature, and codependent adults.

Adolescence is the perfect time to give children a glimpse of what life outside of the comfort of home looks like and allow them to fail and learn in front of your eyes. Sure, your child may kick and scream when the warm and safe bubble bursts and are now expected to learn how to manage their disability. But the upside is that they are developing life skills that will help them build a life on their own once they leave home.

Types of Parents Who Are Prone to Overparenting

It is common to project your own fears and insecurities on your child without even realizing it. For instance, you might restrict your child from staying out late because of your own fears of being out at night. Or, you might warn them against pursuing certain goals because of your own concerns.

You might think that projecting fear onto your child is a way of protecting them from failure. But in reality, projecting fear onto your child makes them afraid of failure and, therefore, reluctant to explore the world. Without your child being made to feel safe leaving their comfort zone, they never will. They'll continue to live in your shadow, waiting for validation that the coast is clear, before making decisions in their life.

There are two types of unhealthy parenting styles that are common among the ASD community. These parenting styles do more damage than good when raising teenagers with autism. The reason for this is because they clip children's wings before they learn how to fly, making them sickly dependent on their parents even beyond adolescence. Go through each parenting style and see whether you can identify some of the behaviors in how you parent your child.

Helicopter Parenting

Helicopter parenting describes the behavior of hovering over your child, constantly monitoring their movements and offering unsolicited help or advice. You may feel anxious when you're not included in your child's school or social affairs; you desire for them to always turn to you and show signs of needing you.

What makes helicopter parenting difficult to spot is the fact that teenagers with autism actually need extra support. For example, you probably have a lot of evidence proving that your child cannot perform certain tasks on their own or needs to be reminded to complete tasks, otherwise they forget. But there's a difference between being supportive and hovering over your child.

The first difference is that support is often requested, not forced upon someone. When you offer support, you are responding to a request for help. Hovering over your child is an invasion of space and privacy; you worm your way into situations that they didn't invite you to and offer unnecessary feedback.

Snowplow Parenting

Snowplow parenting goes a step further than helicopter parenting. It describes the behavior of removing every possible obstacle in your child's path. Forget hovering over them: You step in front of them and direct what they do, where they go, and what they should avoid.

A helicopter parent is clingy and codependent on their child, whereas a snowplow parent is controlling and possessive of their child. A typical example would be drawing up your child's study notes on their behalf because you're worried they won't add the correct information. You might also orchestrate your child's social life by initiating friendships on their behalf. When it's time to fill out college applications, you might spend a weekend completing applications on behalf of your child.

The danger with snowplow parenting is that your child never gets to experience what it's like to struggle, solve problems, or make important decisions for their life. They may also grow up being ignorant of how social systems like banking, healthcare, and the job market work.

While it is understandable why parents would want to help their children cope with the stressors of this world, it is unhealthy to remove stressor altogether. Pulitzer Prize-winner and Novelist Barbara Kingsolver said this about parenting: "Kids don't stay with you if you do it right. It's the one job where, the better you are, the more surely you won't be needed in the long run" (Morin, 2022, para. 3).

As your child grows, your relationship is bound to evolve. They will go from needing you to tie their shoe laces to making plans on their own. You should be proud of yourself as a parent when your child no longer depends on you to follow up after them. It shows their willingness to be independent and wrestle with problems on their own.

Will they always get it right? No, they won't. And that is particularly why your role as a parent is irreplaceable. The truth of the matter is that your child will always need your support and guidance no matter how old they are, but not in the same way they did as a child.

Exercise for Parents: Activities to Build Trust With Your Teen

Building trust with your child allows you to hand over some power in the relationship and feel confident in their ability to exercise it well. Whenever you're not around them, you can rest assured that they are capable of making good decisions and solving their own problems.

If you don't feel like you have reached this point in your relationship with your child, here are a few activities you can practice:

1. **Ask open-ended questions**: The best way to build trust and get to know your child is to show curiosity about their outlook on the world. Encourage your child to share their thoughts and feelings by asking open-ended questions.

2. **Be specific with your praise**: Trust is built through safety and vulnerability. A great way to make your child feel safe expressing themselves is to be specific about the compliments you give them. Learn to notice when your child is performing desirable behavior or revealing a special talent and be the first to praise them!

3. **Be willing to apologize**: If you want a trusting relationship with your child, you will need to model trusting behaviors. A simple and effective behavior to practice is being quick to apologize for your mistakes. This is especially important when you have wronged your child and owe them an apology.

4. **Create opportunities for your child to be independent**: It's better to hand over power than for your child to grab it out of your hands. Deliberately create opportunities for your child to take control and get a feel for independence. For example, you can teach them how to drive, allow them to prepare family meals a few times a week, or let them decide when they want to come back home after a night with friends.

5. **Be their biggest cheerleader**: It is common for teenagers with ASD to feel like the world is against them. However, they shouldn't have any doubts about their parents being on their side. Whenever your child has meltdowns, gets in trouble at school, or behaves in unexplainable ways, reassure them that you are cheering them on. Defend them at school and in front of critical family members or teachers who may not know a lot about ASD.

Exercise for Teens: Activities to Build Trust With Your Parents

Building a trusting relationship with your parents enables you to feel safe expressing your deep thoughts and feelings without fear of being judged or criticized. It also allows you to reach out to your parents for help when you are overwhelmed and feel confident that they will offer you the love and support you need.

If you don't feel like you have reached this point in your relationship with your parents, here are a few activities you can practice:

1. **Be honest and upfront about what you need**: It can be scary to come out and express your needs, especially when you didn't get what you were looking for the last time you tried. Nevertheless, it's important to keep making an effort to communicate what you need from your parents so that they know how to support you. Next time you express your needs, open the dialogue with this statement: "Mom/Dad, I really need something from you right now, and it's taken a lot of courage for me to ask for it. What I need is [need]."

2. **Tell the truth, even if it hurts in the moment**: Those little white lies? Well, they aren't so little in your parents 'world. In order for them to give you space and not interfere too much in your life, they need to know the truth about what you are doing, who you are with, and when you are struggling and need help. Voluntarily give up information about your whereabouts, what you are getting up to, and mistakes you have made, so that your parents don't have to worry when you are out of sight.

3. **Explain how good it feels for them to trust you**: Sometimes your parents don't realize how good it feels when they trust you. Therefore, remind them how amazing it feels to be trusted whenever they loosen their grip a little and give you some control. Take a moment to thank them for trusting you and share how it makes you feel. For instance, you might say, "Mom/Dad, thank you for letting me go to the movies

with my friend. It made me really happy to go by myself and enjoy some freedom."

Chapter 3:

When Naughty Antics Become

Defiant Behavior

Calling a child "rebellious" has the equivalent effect of calling a child that is struggling in school "stupid." It becomes a self-fulfilling prophecy. –Tim Kimmel

Why Do Teenagers Act Out?

The transitions that occur during adolescence are stressful for parents too! Dealing with a grouchy teenager who won't talk about how they are feeling or acts like the boss in the house isn't something that parents are mentally and emotionally prepared for.

When your child's troublesome behaviors catch you off guard, they can negatively impact your well-being and lead to many fights over their bad attitude. To protect yourself from taking their hormone-fueled tantrums personally, it's worth reminding yourself that they're going through a stage that will eventually pass.

It's normal for teenagers to act out during adolescence. As they go through the uncomfortable physical, mental, and emotional changes, they become difficult to discipline and engage with. Your child isn't acting worse than other kids their age; they are being a typical stubborn and egotistical teenager!

You may be asking yourself why they behave this way. We have already touched on the answer to this question in the previous chapter, mentioning that it is normal for teenagers to seek independence and a greater sense of control during adolescence as a way to self-actualize and prepare for adulthood.

However, another useful factor to consider is that your child is wrestling with the existential concept of identity and exploring who they are not in order to reach the discovery of who they are! This may sound strange, but your child needs to act out to explore different kinds of "selves" that they can be. This exercise is crucial to rule out traits that don't sit well with them or bring positive feedback.

Psychoanalyst Erik Erikson came up with a model called the eight psychosocial stages of development (Lewis, 2023). At each stage, beginning from 12 months old and going into adulthood, human beings are confronted with a developmental crisis. Between the ages of 13 and 18—what we refer to as adolescence—young people reach stage five of Erikson's model, which is the "Identity versus Confusion" stage.

The major crisis adolescents encounter at this stage is figuring out who they are and building a stable sense of self. Since there is no formula or manual for building a stable sense of self, young people must step out of their comfort zones and explore. In other words, the training wheels come off and they hit as many walls as they can until they regain balance.

The negative effect of adolescents not building a stable sense of self is becoming confused about who they are and where they fit in the world. Confusion can manifest as developing multiple personalities depending on who they are with, people-pleasing tendencies, anxiety about the future, self-consciousness about physical attributes, and the fear of individuating from parents.

When your child is confronted with this developmental crisis, how do you wish they would respond? Do you desire for them to develop a stable sense of self, or spend a lifetime struggling with identity issues? Of course, as a parent, you want your child to be successful in the world and reach milestones that you can only dream about. However, the only way they can have a successful adult life is if they explore who they are right now.

Erikson believed that offering teenagers positive reinforcement during this stage can support their efforts of building a solid identity. As tough as it will be sometimes, it's important for you to remain positive and hopeful during your child's behavioral highs and lows. Be the stable anchor that they need in this turbulent time and constantly remind them of their strengths. Eventually, they will start to believe in themselves more and voluntarily choose to become the best (not worst) version of themselves.

How to Respond to Bad Behaviors

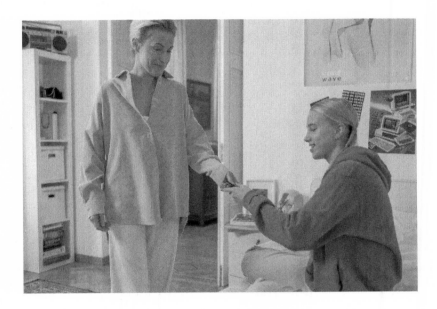

Accepting that it is normal for teenagers to act out doesn't mean that you should tolerate bad behaviors. The reality is that the longer your child is permitted to behave badly, the more ingrained the behavior will be in their mind.

Furthermore, there are consequences to bad behaviors outside of the home, like getting expelled from school or being banned from certain social spots. Thus, to protect your child from hurting themselves and others, it is critical for you to intervene and take action against bad behaviors.

Before you can start addressing your child's bad behaviors, the first step is to understand the intention or unspoken need behind behaving badly. Most (but not all) of the time, your child behaves badly because they don't have knowledge of skills and strategies to manage stress or solve problems. They turn to bad behaviors because it's the quickest and easiest response during a crisis.

Consider a typical scenario where your child storms off after an argument, screaming at the top of their lungs and expressing inaudible words. What do you suppose they are feeling at that moment and struggling to express? Perhaps they are feeling misunderstood but don't have the vocabulary or assertiveness skills to communicate this to you. What has seemed to work in the past—and continues to work right now—is yelling and being impossible to manage. This is their way of showing disapproval for how the situation is going.

Another scenario could be your child skipping the classes that they despise the most. One of the reasons why they might choose to behave this way is that they don't know how else to solve the problem of being overwhelmed in class. Perhaps they dislike the teacher or find it hard to keep up with the pace of the class. Without effective problem-solving skills, they take the easy route and simply avoid going to class altogether.

One of the ways to help your child strive for desirable behaviors and limit bad behaviors is to teach them various coping skills and strategies to practice whenever they are feeling stressed or anxious. Below are examples of common bad behaviors displayed by teens and positive ways you can respond as a parent.

Experimenting With Sex, Drugs, or Alcohol

It's common nowadays, due to the advent of the internet, for teenagers to be exposed to sex, drugs, and alcohol. Even if they are not physically engaged in these activities, they come across content promoting them. Another source of information is their peer group; what they learn from their friends about sex, drugs, and alcohol can influence their desire to experiment with these activities and try it for themselves.

You shouldn't be surprised to come across sexual content on your 13-year-old's browsing history, or smell alcohol on your 15-year-old's breath after a social gathering with friends. Even if you believe that your child isn't participating in these activities, you shouldn't be surprised to learn that their friends or classmates could be.

Solution: Instead of sheltering your child from these realities, take the opportunity to educate them on what they are, how they are used, and possible dangers that could come from them. Offer a balanced perspective, weighing the pros and cons of engaging in sex, drugs, and alcohol, then leave the final decision or conclusion for your child to form.

Make it clear to them that the choice to engage in these activities is solely theirs to make. However, they should understand the consequences of participating in these activities, such as potentially becoming pregnant or developing a substance abuse problem.

Dependency on Social Media and Technological Devices

A study conducted at the University of Wisconsin School of Medicine and Public Health found that teenagers who are at a higher risk of developing depression, body issues, and the "fear of missing out" reported higher rates of personal ownership of a technological device (University of Wisconsin, 2022).

It is alarming how much young people depend on technology—particularly their cell phones—to connect with the world. Having such an unhealthy relationship with technology can negatively impact their sleep cycles, productivity, and social connectedness. Moreover, relying on social media for information can lead to a warped sense of reality, where teens believe that curated and photoshopped content is aspirational and achievable.

Solution: It's rare to find any parent who is happy with their child's technology consumption. But creating strict rules around technology or confiscating devices doesn't seem to break the unhealthy patterns.

A better approach when addressing technology dependency and social media usage is to encourage open dialogue around the benefits and risks of using technology, as well as negotiate healthy limits that both you and your child can commit to.

Explain to your child how being online all the time can aggravate their anxiety or create self-esteem issues. Use case studies to illustrate how technology usage can be addictive and damaging on a psychological level. Balance the risks with opportunities to use technology and how various apps, social media groups, or blog sites can help your child develop a positive self-image.

The most important part, however, is teaching your child problem-solving skills by brainstorming and planning healthier ways to engage with technology. Reassure them that you're happy for them to use technology, but only to a certain extent. Discuss what healthy usage looks like to the both of you and create an adjustable routine. On a regular basis, check in to see how the routine is working and any concerns or positive feedback your child may have.

Frequent Unexplained Mood Swings

Even though mood swings are common in teenagers, it isn't behavior that you should normalize. Mood swings are a sign of *repressed emotions*, strong and entangled emotions that your child is feeling. When these emotions aren't given the chance to flow out freely, they can get stronger and deeper and lead to mood disorders like depression.

Mood swings can also negatively impact your child's relationships. When they're in a bad mood, they may not be able to communicate effectively, which makes it difficult for them to socialize with others and maintain positive relationships with teachers and classmates. Building relationships requires a degree of openness in order to share personal experiences with others, as well as to validate the experiences of others.

Solution: Whenever your child experiences mood swings, see this as an opportunity to connect. What they need most (and possibly struggle to express) is someone to talk to about what they're thinking or feeling. For a typical teenager who doesn't yet know how to assert their needs, asking for connection may be tough. However, as their parent, you can pick up on this need and plan to have quality time together.

From experience, you may already know that asking the question "What's wrong?" doesn't get you very far. This type of question can come across as confrontational and make your child feel put on the spot. Instead of being too direct, focus on creating an emotionally safe environment for your child to open up. This means avoiding judgmental words, tones of voice, behaviors, or anything that might cause your child to feel invalidated.

An emotionally safe environment is light, comforting, and accepting. It's the kind of atmosphere that makes you want to daydream, think creatively, or share your deepest desires. Note that sometimes being at home doesn't make your child feel emotionally safe due to the dynamics between family members and other factors. Therefore, to encourage them to open up, consider visiting your child's favorite social scene or perform an activity they enjoy.

When Should You Draw the Line as a Parent?

Talking through bad behavior works, but only sometimes. When your child becomes defiant, such as refusing to engage with you or participate in conflict resolution, simply talking won't help you correct bad behavior.

Due to their challenges with regulating their emotions, your child may become easily angered, irritable, vindictive, or argumentative. These behaviors can be difficult to manage using normal techniques like enforcing a time out or taking away privileges. You may even be afraid of being in your child's presence when they have a meltdown.

Nevertheless, you can't make allowances for these kinds of aggressive behaviors. Not only can they make your child an unpleasant person to be around, but they can get your child into serious trouble at school or with law enforcement. Before we speak about the solution, let's look at what we mean by *defiant behaviors* so that you have a better understanding of where to draw the line. Below are typical signs of defiance to look out for:

- Refusing to follow instructions, like completing homework

- Refusing to spend time with the family or participate in family events

- Using intimidation tactics to frighten parents

- No concern for facing consequences or getting in trouble with authority

- Difficulty controlling temper tantrums

- Becoming easily irritated when they don't get their way

- Impulsive behavior like slamming their bedroom door

- Experimenting with addictive substances

- Difficulty maintaining positive relationships with siblings, parents, school teachers, and classmates

- Displaying antisocial behavior like stealing or cheating without fear of being caught

- Deliberately saying or doing hurtful things to get back at others

What's worth remembering about defiant behaviors is that they challenge the existing rules and structures put in place by parents to create a safe environment. In many cases, a defiant child doesn't have issues with the rules and structure at home per se, but what they might represent.

For example, if your child feels emotionally invalidated as a result of unfair house rules, they will push back in protest as a way of communicating to you their disapproval of your expectations. Pushback can also be a way for your child to express their anger or resentment toward the family dynamics at home, real issues like domestic or substance abuse which are shoved under the rug, or feeling emotionally neglected.

There is almost always a deeper and more heartfelt reason why your child is being defiant. They wouldn't go to such extreme lengths to hurt themselves or others if there wasn't something serious affecting their emotional well-being. Being difficult could be your child's way of getting your attention.

Perhaps they have been trying to communicate the same message over and over again but haven't been successful at getting through to you. Or maybe they feel afraid to come out and express their strong emotions, so they find aggressive ways to release them. Either way, defiant behavior should be seen and treated as a cry for help; a moment to stop whatever you're busy with and attend to your child's unspoken needs.

The Process of Diagnosing Oppositional Defiant Disorder

Teenagers with ASD are particularly vulnerable to developing oppositional defiant disorder (ODD). This medical condition is characterized by extreme and uncontrollable anger issues. It is often diagnosed as a comorbidity in people who suffer from disorders like autism or attention-deficit hyperactivity disorder (ADHD), where executive functions like being able to make good judgment and control impulses are damaged.

Of course, not every teenager on the spectrum will develop ODD. The probability of getting this condition depends on social, biological, and psychological factors. For example, if there is a history of ODD, ASD, or ADHD in the family, or issues with substance abuse, then the risk gets higher. Other contributing factors include the lack of parental supervision, consistent and positive discipline, and a stable and nurturing household environment.

When examining teenagers for signs of ODD, medical doctors normally look for a pattern of irritability, mood swings, and defiant behaviors. The young person must display at least four of the following symptoms for at least six months. The symptoms are summarized in the acronym REAL BADS (PsychDB, 2021):

R: Resentful

E: Easily annoyed

A: Argues with adults

L: Loses temper

B: Blames others

A: Annoys people deliberately

D: Defies rules or requests

S: Spiteful

Doctors will also consider the severity of the symptoms. For example, if the young person only shows signs of ODD in one setting, such as at home or at school, the symptoms are considered mild. If the young person shows signs of ODD in two separate settings, the symptoms are considered moderate. Severe symptoms occur when signs of ODD appear in three or more settings.

Treatment for ODD includes a combination of behavioral therapy and parents training. Family therapy can also be a good way to help affected family members learn how to relate to one another, manage stress, and communicate in healthier ways.

Why Traditional Discipline Doesn't Work on a Teenager With Autism Spectrum Disorder

The purpose of disciplining your child is to teach them the difference between acceptable and unacceptable behaviors. Traditional forms of discipline like grounding, taking away privileges, or instilling fear are not effective in helping teenagers with autism learn and practice desirable behaviors.

For example, if you take away a privilege from your child after they have crossed a boundary, they will feel more hurt from being deprived of their favorite pastime activity than recognizing the inappropriateness of their behavior.

The same applies when you instill fear in your child or become physically aggressive. Their mind is unable to connect the punishment to the crime. All they remember is the pain of the punishment and the seemingly unjustified cruelty of their parents.

There are three valid explanations for why traditional discipline doesn't work on your child.

Impaired Executive Function

There are a few skills that don't come easy for your child, such as memorizing information, self-regulating, and impulse control. This means that when you discipline your child, there is a high chance they will commit the same behavior again. More punishments therefore don't bring positive changes to behavior; only positive reinforcement and consistency can.

Difficulty Being Others-Minded

Teenagers on the spectrum have difficulty perceiving reality from another person's perspective. As a result, they struggle to empathize with other people, pick up on social cues, or sense when their behavior is making others uncomfortable. When being corrected for their behavior, they can feel surprised or ambushed, not being aware of the far-reaching implications of their actions.

Traditional discipline can therefore feel unfair to children with ASD. The aggressive tone of voice or drastic consequences may seem too harsh and uncalled for. Instead of using the discipline as a teachable moment, they might shut down, withdraw, or become argumentative.

Weak Central Coherence

You will notice that your child tends to focus on the details rather than the bigger picture of a situation. For instance, when you are upset at them for spilling juice on the floor and not cleaning it up, they might say something like, "It was a small drop." They may not stop to consider how the small drop of juice might dry up and cause ants, creating an even bigger issue.

The term used to describe the cognitive ability to pay attention to minor and major aspects of a situation is *central coherence*. Children with ASD are known to have a weak central coherence, which means that they tend to focus on specific details and miss the big picture. This could explain why they may feel confused when questioned about their bad behavior or given what seems to be harsh consequences. They need help being shown how one action might lead to a bigger action, or how something so small can have a big and long-lasting impact.

Direct, Clear, and Impactful Discipline for Teens With Autism

What often works for teens on the spectrum is clear, direct, and impactful discipline. Being clear and direct allows your child to understand why they are in trouble without misconstruing your words. It may also be easier for them to draw a connection between their behavior and breaking rules or crossing boundaries.

Impactful discipline is about making the consequence bold, so much so that your child is forced to pause and rethink their actions. Instead of aiming to punish your child, strive to leave a lasting impression in their mind by doing something significant.

The following strategies can help you practice clear, direct, and impactful discipline.

Control Only What You Can: Yourself

Remind yourself that you cannot control your child's behaviors; only they can do that. If they choose to yell, hurl insults, or deliberately seek to provoke you, there is little you can do to make the behavior stop. Nonetheless, you have complete control over how you choose to govern your thoughts, feelings, and actions at that moment.

Focusing on yourself can be a great distraction from defiant behaviors. It can also give you an opportunity to breathe and regulate your own impulses. The shift away from your child's bad behavior and onto your own well-being can send a clear, direct, and impactful message that your state of mind and peace is more important than their aggressive behavior.

Remember that there is always an unspoken need behind misbehaving, which could be seeking out your attention. When you don't give away your attention to negative behaviors, your child will start to find other ways to grab it. They quickly learn that being difficult isn't a good strategy to get Mom or Dad to listen. In fact, it makes Mom or Dad shut off.

Allow Natural Consequences

If you want to take back your power as a parent whenever your child is being defiant, allow natural consequences to take place. *Natural consequences* are the universal effects of behaving poorly that occur on their own. You don't need to enforce a natural consequence; you simply need to step back and allow your child to face the reality of their choices.

Take a moment and think: What is the natural consequence of not doing homework? That's right: A zero for the assignment. And what is the natural consequence of disrespecting your parents? Yes: They aren't as willing and enthusiastic about treating you to gifts or saying yes to special requests.

When you allow natural consequences to take place, your child learns the hard way what happens when certain actions are taken. A defiant teenager may need to have this brutal wake up call (or many of them) to realize that unless they change their behaviors, they will continue to stumble.

Be Consistent

Teenagers with autism learn through consistent reinforcement of rules and boundaries. They need to be reminded of their limits on a regular basis. To avoid coming off controlling or nagging, find nonverbal ways to communicate boundaries, leaving the option to follow them in your child's hands.

For example, kitchen chalkboards and rewards charts can be a great way to visually display boundaries and consequences. They can also be used as a way to publicly announce rewards or privileges for good behavior.

Another aspect of consistency is being true to your word and implementing the same consequences whenever certain boundaries are crossed. The aim is to create a structured approach to discipline that feels predictable and makes it easy to choose desirable behaviors over and over again.

Be Mindful of Consequences

Teenagers who are on the spectrum are so used to being reprimanded that they can sometimes go numb to consequences. To avoid exhausting your child and making your discipline ineffective, learn different ways to approach your child's behaviors.

For example, you can create a list of behaviors you consider defiant and unacceptable. Thereafter, draw a table and categorize each behavior under mild, moderate, and severe defiance. For each category, think of consequences that are suitable for the behavior. The consequences should also range in severity.

Keep this table somewhere accessible, like on your cell phone's notepad, so you can refer back to it whenever you need a refresher. Remember to be consistent when enforcing these consequences to help your child distinguish between mild, moderate, and severe defiant behaviors.

Exercise for Parents: Help Your Teen Identify and Respectfully Express Their Feelings

Take a moment to reflect on this idea: If your child knew how to behave appropriately, they would.

When the option of pleasure is available, nobody chooses pain. Bad behavior should therefore be seen as a sign of not knowing how to act appropriately. A major barrier to acting appropriately is not knowing how to express strong emotions in a productive way.

You can make it easier for your child to behave well by teaching them emotional regulation skills. These are skills that enable your child to identify, name, and describe their emotions without acting them out. The benefit of learning emotional regulation skills is that they help your child feel more in control of their feelings during stressful times.

Below are a few exercises to teach your child.

Step One: Tuning in to Body Cues

Teach your child to listen to their body whenever they're feeling off balance. Encourage them to track different bodily sensations, such as sharpness, tightness, heaviness, or heat/cold. Which body parts are these sensations coming from?

On a scale of 1 to 10, how intense are the sensations? Ask them to put all of this information in a sentence, like, "I feel tightness in my chest, and it's a 6 out of 10." Decide on a specific rating they must reach to approach you and share what they are experiencing. For example, both of you might decide that when a sensation reaches 8.5 out of 10, your child needs to find you or call you and share what they are feeling.

Step Two: Connecting Sensations to Emotions

Once you have taught your child how to pick up on bodily sensations, the next step is to teach them the connection between sensations and emotions. To make it easier for your child, identify common body sensations they feel in common body parts. This could be a tightness in the chest.

Thereafter, provide your child with a few different emotions that might explain the body sensation. For example, the tightness in the chest could be a result of being afraid, nervous, surprised, sad, or disappointed.

Go through each emotion and ask your child to describe how different the tightness would feel if that was what they were experiencing. Does fear cause a mild, moderate, or severe tightness? What about being surprised? Ask your child to rate the level of tightness of each emotion on the same scale.

Write this information down somewhere so that your child can visually see what emotions they may be experiencing as the intensity of their sensations increase.

Step Three: Connecting Behaviors to Emotions

Another exercise to teach your child is to recognize the emotions behind their behaviors. The fact is that behaviors don't come from midair. They are an expression of an emotion. For instance, when you're happy, you tend to smile, but when you're upset, you tend to spend more time alone.

This is an ongoing exercise that will require keeping a diary. Challenge your child to track the emotions behind five behaviors (bonus points if they can identify the body sensations they experience when the emotion arises).

Give them a reward for their hard work, then increase the stakes and ask them to track another five behaviors and so on until they have a table of 50 behaviors and the emotions behind them. Dish out rewards after each small challenge to keep your child motivated!

Exercise for Teens: Self-Soothing Techniques That Can Quieten the Inner Storm

When you are upset and feel as though you're about to explode, it's the perfect time to retreat to a quiet place and self-soothe.

Self-soothing is the process of comforting yourself to reduce stress. Your focus shifts away from whatever situation is frustrating you and onto your well-being. When you're tuned into what you are thinking and feeling, you can gradually calm yourself down and restore harmony inside your body.

What's great about self-soothing is that you don't need to rely on other people or circumstances to make you feel better. You can become your own source of encouragement to get through the difficult times!

There are various techniques that can help you self-soothe. Below are a few you can practice:

- **Write it out**: Do you have a lot on your mind but aren't sure how to express what you're feeling? Journaling is one of the best exercises to relieve stress and help you make sense of your thoughts and feelings.

- **Draw something**: Being creative has a calming effect on the brain. Whenever you're overwhelmed, try expressing your mental or emotional state through drawings and other types of artwork.

- **Play music**: Musical melodies and touching song lyrics have a way of soothing your mind and speaking to your emotional side. Create several themed playlists with songs that speak on different emotions, such as anger, fear, happiness, and peace.

- **Take a deep breath**: Slowing down and regulating your breathing has a calming effect on your mind and body. The more oxygen you inhale, the more relaxed you feel. Practice this simple exercise: Slowly inhale through your nose for five counts, hold your breath for five counts, gently exhale through your mouth for five counts, then repeat the sequence.

- **Make a list of the positives**: Did you know that the human brain is more prone to thinking negatively? A simple way to uplift your mood is to create a gratitude list and focus on the positive things that are happening in your life. Challenge yourself to think of as many small and big wins as you can!

- **Change your body temperature**: When you're upset, your body temperature tends to increase. A quick way to manage your stress levels is to bring your temperature back down. For instance, you can run your hands or splash your face with extremely cold water, take a cold shower or dip in the pool, or place an ice pack on your forehead or eyes for 15–30 seconds.

Chapter 4:

How to Help Your Teen

Manage School Demands and

Prepare for College

I'm not telling you it's going to be easy—I'm telling you it's going to be worth it. —Art Williams

Why Is High School Difficult When You Have Autism Spectrum Disorder?

Are you concerned about your child's attitude toward school? Their disinterest when it comes to studying for tests? Or what may come across as a general lack of effort in their school work?

Laziness is a word that is often used to describe a teenager with autism's approach to school. While it's true that some are lazy when it comes to completing school work and applying themselves, many teenagers with autism are misunderstood as being lazy due to their cognitive, social, and sensory challenges that affect their experience in a school environment.

For a young person with ASD, high school is a stress and anxiety-triggering environment for multiple reasons. First, many public high schools are not built to cater to the needs of students with autism. This means that the classroom atmosphere, structure of the lessons, and pace of learning do not accommodate students with sensory sensitivities or cognitive impairments.

Imagine feeling overwhelmed from the moment you got to school in the morning until the moment you left for home. At random moments throughout the day, you were triggered by the lighting, loud voices, confusing class assignments, and being yelled at by a teacher in front of everybody for reasons you didn't quite understand. And then there are the peer dynamics that throw you off balance and feel like a never-ending battle to gain acceptance from classmates and try by all means to fit in.

This is just a glimpse of a typical school day for a teenager with ASD. They are constantly bombarded with information that is difficult to break down, process, and understand. Not only that, but they are also conscious of the fact that they're different from other children, and this can trigger fears of not being good enough and not belonging at that particular high school.

By the time your child reaches adolescence, they have overcome many of the reading, writing, and comprehension difficulties. They may even have useful hacks to stay organized, manage time, and stay on top of their work flow. Nevertheless, there are still adjustments that they need to make to keep up with the increasing pace of school demands and become more independent in managing their schedule and completing tasks.

If you were previously involved in every aspect of your child's school life, now is the period to slowly start stepping back and giving your child more control over their work. Remember that after high school is either college or the beginning of your child's work career. Your challenge as a parent is to do the best you can during these six years to prepare them for an independent and successful educational or professional career.

Autism and School Anxiety

Feeling anxious about school isn't an excuse for your child to bunk class. Sure, it may sound really convenient that they express feeling anxious about going to school right before a test, but the truth is that there are some real fears behind their anxiety, which you can help them work through.

There are three valid explanations for why your child may feel anxious thinking about school or preparing to go to school. These include

- difficult relationships with peers and school teachers,

- unspoken expectations about classroom etiquette and how to carry out work tasks, and

- unexpected changes that require them to adapt on the spot, making them feel out of control.

Besides academic performance, the social aspect of high school can be daunting for your child. Perhaps due to past experiences of being bullied, alienated, or criticized by students and teachers, they are less open to building relationships and may prefer to spend time alone.

To cope with their real or perceived history of social rejection, your child may develop negative assumptions about specific types or general groups of people. For example, they might believe that the "popular kids" are mean airheads, the English teacher is unfair, and the opposite gender is confusing and should be avoided at all cost!

The combination of these problems create a tendency of overthinking and jumping to the worst conclusions about school life. Instead of applying their minds to adapt to school demands, your child may become preoccupied with finding reasons why they dislike school, certain subjects, or certain people. What drives their preoccupation with the negative aspects of school is feeling anxious and unprepared for the environment they are stepping into.

Ways to Help Your Child Manage School Anxiety

It's important to make a distinction between helping your child manage school anxiety and trying to protect them against things that might cause them to feel anxious. The latter would lead to controlling and overbearing behaviors.

The reality is that many teenagers, whether they are diagnosed with ASD or not, will have negative thoughts and feelings about school. The same can be said about how some adults have negative perceptions about their jobs, parenting, or taking care of their elderly parents.

Your child's anxious feelings about school aren't something that you can fix. However, you can step in and teach them various ways to manage their anxiety. Make it a point to tell your child that there will be many times in life when they are required to do things they dislike, but don't have an option to pull out of those responsibilities. For the time being, school is a compulsory obligation, but in a few years, it will be college or a full-time job.

Encourage your child to shift their focus from thinking about what might go wrong to considering what might go well. Sure, it may take more effort to focus on the positives, but with practice, your child can slowly improve their attitude toward school. Below are a few more valuable strategies that can help your child manage school anxiety.

Creating an Ultimate School Day Morning Routine

How your child starts the day can have a great impact on their state of mind and attitude throughout the day. Encourage your child to create an ultimate morning routine consisting of positive and productive activities to start the day on a high note. Some of the activities that can be included in the routine are meditation, reading a book, eating a healthy breakfast, and playing outside with your pets.

Setting Positive Intentions for the Day

Another productive activity to complete in the morning is setting positive intentions for the day. These are statements that express your child's aspirations for the day, such as how they want to feel in class or how they desire social interactions to go.

In a notebook, ask your child to write down three positive experiences they aspire to have each day. Later on in the evening, remind them to reflect on how close they came to fulfilling their aspirations.

Being Comfortable Asking for Help

One of the causes of anxiety is not being clear about school rules and expectations. For example, your child might dislike a certain subject because they don't understand what the teacher expects from them. Summoning the courage to ask for help at school can alleviate a lot of your child's anxiety.

Take the time to highlight a few benefits of asking for help, such as gaining clarity and being able to submit good work, to show your child why they should strive to perform this behavior. You can also teach them different scenarios where asking for help will and won't get them in trouble, and provide a few scripts that they can use when making a request to a friend or teacher.

For instance, asking for help won't get them into trouble when they don't understand an instruction and need the teacher to explain it in a different way. However, asking for help can get them into trouble if the teacher has already given the answer to the question they are asking (the teacher will be upset because it shows that your child wasn't paying attention while they were speaking).

There are also different ways to ask for help, such as saying:

- "Thank you for the explanation. I understand what to do up until this point,but after that, I'm confused about what to do."

- "I don't understand why [insert scenario here]. May you please explain it to me?"

- "May you please give me some advice on how to approach this task?"

- "I have tried [method 1] and [method 2], but I can't seem to get it right. Am I following the instructions correctly?"

Teach your child to get into the habit of asking for help before the very last minute. Similarly to how they would rate the intensity of their emotions on a scale, show them how to rate their level of confusion honestly and seek help immediately.

Another healthy habit is for your child to review homework assignments before going home (maybe during break time) so that they can approach their teachers with questions about the assignments and clear any confusion.

Role Play Common School Social Interactions

Your child may not be getting bullied at school, but they could have fears or doubts about social interactions. The last thing any teenager with ASD wants is to embarrass themselves, especially without even knowing it!

It can be fun and helpful to walk your child through different social interactions they may have at school. The purpose of this is to help them plan in advance how they might approach the situation and reduce as much anxiety as possible. Examples of social interactions you can reenact include

- greeting a new acquaintance in class

- greeting a school teacher in the corridor

- apologizing for making a mistake

- showing interest in other people

- expressing a personal boundary

- reading nonverbal body language and behaving accordingly

- expressing likes and dislikes and turning the conversation to others

- validating other people's thoughts, even when they have different opinions

When role playing, both of you should get into character, your child playing themselves in that particular situation and you playing the other individual. Switch up the scenarios to provide as many variations as possible, such as the best and worst-case scenarios. Make the exercise fun by rewarding your child for every interaction they handle well. Repetition is key when teaching a skill to a child with ASD, so make time to role play at least once every week!

Have the Conversation About Higher Education

During the teenage years, it's important to regularly bring up the conversation about plans after high school. The traditional route that many kids take is to apply for college or university. However, that isn't the only option available, and it's worth familiarizing your child with the various routes they could take.

Due to the enormous amounts of challenges teenagers with autism face at school, it is not uncommon for them to be hesitant to pursue higher education. For instance, your child may have a negative perception about college based on rumors they have heard or generalizations they've made. As their parent, you can educate them on the facts about this big decision and see whether it's something they truly desire or not.

Before selling the idea of college to your child, it is worth validating some of the concerns they may have. There are valid reasons why they may be fearful or opposed to pursuing higher education. The first is true for every teenager: Not everybody is built for or has the desire to attend a college. Your child may simply not be interested in going the formal route of learning. Furthermore, their passions may not require them to have a college degree, thereby making formal education unnecessary.

The second reason has a lot to do with their cognitive disabilities. Let's face it: To succeed at a tertiary institution, you will need to learn and master critical thinking (it may also help to have good time management, multitasking, and planning skills). Due to executive function impairments, it could be very hard for your child to adjust to the demands of college life, making them feel overwhelmed by tasks that other students may be comfortable with.

Thirdly, pursuing higher education requires a great deal of independence. As a college student, for example, you are expected to stay up-to-date with deadlines, submit your work correctly and on time, attend tutoring sessions, and actively seek help when you don't understand something. The need for independence can also spill over to a student's living arrangements, financial management, and social life. With greater freedom comes more responsibilities, and this could be something your child isn't prepared for, as of yet.

It's also worth exploring whether your child genuinely wants to pursue higher education, or if it is something they feel forced to do. Society has a way of depicting what it believes to be the ideal route to success, and most times this begins with attending a tertiary institution and getting a degree. Based on the conversations your child has with their friends, or content they watch on social media, they may feel pressured to go the route of college simply because they want to fit in.

Without having a genuine desire to go to college, it can be difficult for your child to withstand and adjust to the many challenges they might encounter at that level. Plus, those three to four years spent studying toward a degree that doesn't feel meaningful can delay them from actually finding purposeful work. It is true that for most of their childhood, your child has felt different. But after leaving high school, being different becomes a strength, not a weakness.

There are many examples of successful inventors, artists, and entrepreneurs who built businesses and transformed society without having gone to college or dropped out after a semester. They were undoubtedly different from everybody else and chose an unconventional path, but because they focused on their passions, they were able to become influential.

Steve Jobs attended Reed College in Portland for only a semester before dropping out. He took a study break and traveled to India, where he explored other interests unrelated to school, such as his spirituality. Upon his return, Jobs was motivated to start a business centered around his interest in computers. He convinced a good friend, Steve Wozniak, to be a business partner, and that is how the company Apple was formed.

Anna Wintour is another great example of a successful woman who got ahead without a college degree. She has been the editor-in-chief of American Vogue magazine since 1988 and has helped make it the success it is today. After dropping out from the North London Collegiate School, she decided to pursue a career in fashion. Wintour started from the bottom, working as an editorial assistant and junior fashion editor for various magazines, until she eventually landed the job of creative director at Vogue.

As you can tell, success, broadly speaking, may or may not involve pursuing higher education. This is something that your child may be pleased to know. Nevertheless, it also doesn't mean that learning stops after high school. There are a few alternatives to attending college that can prepare your child for a successful career!

Explore the Alternatives for Going to College

There are some teens on the spectrum who are excited about one day going to college, and others who would prefer exploring alternatives to traditional tertiary education. They aren't necessarily running away from the challenges of college; they are simply looking for after-school learning that matches their interests.

It can be a fun exercise to explore various alternatives to college with your child. Not only can you learn more about who they are and what they are passionate about, but you can also play a crucial role in offering mentorship.

Whatever occupation your child envisions for themselves will require skills and knowledge. Therefore, pursuing advanced education is a must for a successful career. Nonetheless, not every occupation requires formal training, which means that your child can decide how they structure their learning after high school.

Below are some alternatives that you can present to your child to get a conversation started.

Vocational Training and Trade Schools

Vocational training equips your child with the necessary skills to enter a specific trade or craft. The focus is on teaching your child practical career-related skills to help them specialize in a particular field. For example, you can find trade schools for engineering, tourism and hospitality, culinary arts, hairdressing, beauty therapy, fashion design, or mechanical trades like plumbing, welding, or carpentry.

This option is suitable for your child if they have expressed interest in a specific trade. For instance, culinary school could be a great choice for a young person who identifies as a foodie and enjoys cooking. Another young person who enjoys the art of makeup and experimenting with beauty products might succeed at a beauty therapy school.

Trade schools are typically more affordable than traditional colleges or universities, which means that you can save thousands of dollars in tuition, depending on your child's specialty and school that you choose.

Self-Paced Learning

Perhaps your child's biggest issue with traditional school is the pace of learning. They may often miss deadlines or run out of time to complete tests. The speed of learning can make it difficult for them to focus and understand the work in front of them. Instead of going to college, they might prefer taking up a course that allows them to learn at their own pace.

Self-paced learning is often packaged as paid or free online courses that equip you with specific skills. Most paid courses are accredited by formal institutions or companies and come with a certificate of completion at the end. This means that they are counted as legitimate educational qualifications.

Similar to vocational training, courses are structured to teach specific skills. Based on your child's interests, they can take up a course about coding, graphic design, artificial intelligence, or psychology. Courses make it easy to specialize in a specific area within a larger career field. For instance, within the coding niche, your child may focus on learning a specific coding language.

Self-paced learning is suitable for your child if they desire to develop skills at their own pace without time pressure or a rigid schedule. They may even want to start working part-time to gain career experience while completing a series of courses on the side.

Apprenticeship

There are some occupations that provide on-the-job or on-site training. In general, these occupations tend to be trades that require you to complete specific tasks. Apprenticeships are skills-based work opportunities that focus on training junior practitioners with the relevant knowledge to complete a job. Most of the skills and knowledge are taught through hands-on, practical learning.

Apprenticeships are often seen as legitimate educational experience, which can count toward obtaining a license to practice within a field. Research shows that people who enter apprenticeship programs are paid between 50% and 60% of what full-time tradesmen earn (Galarita, 2023). For a young person straight out of high school, this salary is often enough to pay living expenses. As they gain more experience and become proficient at their trade, their salary will be adjusted accordingly.

Another advantage of apprenticeships is that some partner with trade schools and community colleges. The experience you gain on the job can count toward college credits. This means that by taking up an apprenticeship, your child can potentially qualify for a college certificate or reduce the number of years spent working toward a degree.

Joining the Military

There are plenty of educational opportunities offered by the military. Depending on the area of service that appeals to your child, they can get free access to different types of training programs. Joining the military can also help your child learn soft skills, such as how to communicate effectively, solve problems, adapt to different environments, and so on.

The military also provides opportunities abroad or in multiple locations across the country. If your child enjoys traveling and exploring different cultures, they can apply for military short-term positions in different places. Some colleges count military experience toward obtaining a college degree. This means that when your child is ready to leave the military and start a formal career, they will have some college credits already. The state also provides financial aid and benefits to ex-military members who need funding for college.

Entrepreneurship

Another viable option for your child is starting a business. They could have a special interest or hobby that has potential to become a profitable product or service. Even though a traditional degree is not required to enter entrepreneurship, your child will need to develop certain skills to run their business effectively. These skills can be cultivated through on-the-job training, self-paced learning, or spending a few years at a trade school.

Alternatively, if you are a business owner or know of a close friend or family member who runs a business, you can arrange for your child to become an apprentice and work closely with different employees within the organization to learn what they do. This experience will help them gain valuable skills and understand how to set up and operate a successful business.

Exercise for Parents: Help Your Child Improve Their Attitude Toward School

As a parent, you play a significant role in helping your teen successfully get through high school and make the right educational and career choices. Without even saying a word, your actions and attitudes can help them learn how to manage stress, adapt to difficult circumstances, and remain open to learning outside of the classroom.

Teenagers usually deal with stressors similar to those experienced by adults. For example, your child may be complaining about a teacher they dislike, which is similar to how an adult would complain about a difficult supervisor. To prepare your child to face the real world with a can-do attitude, you can teach them how to respond to current stressors like high school in a productive way.

Here are three ways to positively change your child's attitude about school:

1. **Show respect and kindness toward their teachers**: Make it a point to speak positively about their teachers (even the ones you or your child dislike) and show kindness whenever you see them. This teaches your child how to empathize with others, even with people they may disagree with.

2. **Deal with school conflict constructively**: Have a logical and calm approach to resolving problems your child may face at school. Instead of passing blame and making accusations, focus on the facts and seek to reach win-win solutions. This teaches your child how to

communicate effectively and solve problems without jeopardizing relationships.

3. **Encourage self-reflection**: Adopt the habit of reflecting on your own attitudes and behaviors at home. Whenever you make mistakes, offend your child, or react inappropriately, publicly own up to your actions, offer an apology, and discuss what you can do differently next time. This teaches your child to view moments when they step out of character as learning opportunities instead of something to be ashamed of.

Exercise for Teens: Create Your Own Daily Routine

One of the uncomfortable truths about being a teenager is having to juggle more responsibilities. For example, instead of only thinking about waking up and going to school, like you did in middle school, you need to think about

- catching up on homework

- submitting assignments each week and on time

- maintaining a social life (or perhaps building one)

- spending time with family

- getting enough sleep

- staying on top of personal care and hygiene

Creating a daily routine is about taking back control of your day and deciding what's worth your time and what isn't. Without having a predictable routine, you can easily forget to check off important tasks during the day.

The most effective routines are not overloaded with tasks. They consist of the most important tasks of the day, usually five tasks that offer the most value (Burkeman, 2015).

Included is a template for a daily routine. Fill out the empty blocks with priority tasks for each day. Challenge yourself to only include five priority tasks a day. Leave out mandatory tasks like sleeping and eating, and focus on responsibilities you need to take up.

Remember that your priority tasks can change on a daily or weekly basis, depending on new school assignments, sports fixtures, social events, or goals you're working on. Therefore, be flexible enough to adjust how you spend your time. For example, you may need to complete homework at a later time on a specific day because you need to attend a doctor's visit after school.

Time	Task	Notes about the task	Priority ranking	Finished (only tick this column when you have completed each task).
6:00 a.m.				
6:30 a.m.				
7:00 a.m.				
7:30 a.m.				

Time	Task	Notes about the task	Priority ranking	Finished (only tick this column when you have completed each task).
8:00 a.m.				
8:30 a.m.				
9:00 a.m.				
9:30 a.m.				

Time	Task	Notes about the task	Priority ranking	Finished (only tick this column when you have completed each task).
10:00 a.m.				
10:30 a.m.				
11:00 a.m.				
11:30 a.m.				

Time	Task	Notes about the task	Priority ranking	Finished (only tick this column when you have completed each task).
12:00 p.m.				
12:30 p.m.				
1:00 p.m.				
1:30 p.m.				

Time	Task	Notes about the task	Priority ranking	Finished (only tick this column when you have completed each task).
2:00 p.m.				
2:30 p.m.				
3:00 p.m.				
3:30 p.m.				

Time	Task	Notes about the task	Priority ranking	Finished (only tick this column when you have completed each task).
4:00 p.m.				
4:30 p.m.				
5:00 p.m.				
5:30 p.m.				

Time	Task	Notes about the task	Priority ranking	Finished (only tick this column when you have completed each task).
6:00 p.m.				

Chapter 5

Motivate Your Teen to

Dream—How to Help Your

Child Set Goals and Envision a

Bright Future

Never give up on what you really want to do. The person with big dreams is more powerful than one with all the facts. –Albert Einstein

Self-Esteem Issues in Teens With Autism Spectrum Disorder

It's common for teenagers to go through periods of having low self-esteem. This happens because they are still figuring out who they are and what fundamental values and attributes to build their identity on. Since exploration is a big part of this process, teenagers can sometimes latch onto the wrong values and attributes and have a distorted perception of themselves.

A typical example is a young person who bases their identity on performance in multiple domains, such as academics, sports, and social life. Their failure or success in performing in these areas determines how they feel about themselves. Both teens with ASD and those without experience this identity confusion and can go for years thinking poorly of themselves because of not achieving their performance goals.

Low self-esteem issues that are specific to adolescents with ASD stem from feelings of insecurity about their differences from other children their age. They're aware of their cognitive or behavioral limitations and, at the back of their minds, fear not being able to fit in.

Another common problem that may occur from their self-consciousness is the habit of thinking negatively about themselves and their future prospects. For example, a young person on the spectrum might assume that just because they are not coping with the demands of school, they will struggle to build a career and gain independence as a young adult. Or, they might assume that just because they have few to no friends in high school, they will become a lonely and isolated adult and may even struggle to find a romantic partner.

Negative thinking is a self-destructive habit that can warp your child's reality and attack their sense of self-worth. What makes negative thinking difficult to identify and challenge is that most of the time those thoughts sound rational. For example, your child might take the facts of their situation and look at them through a negative lens. This isn't necessarily wrong, but it is one-sided.

In every circumstance, there's a positive and negative outlook that can be adopted. Negative thinkers tend to be biased toward the negative outlook. This causes them to see only half of the picture, not the whole thing. Likewise, when your child adopts a negative outlook on life, they only acknowledge a portion of what is occurring, which isn't enough to form fair and balanced opinions and beliefs about their life.

If you're concerned that your child may be dealing with low self-esteem, the first thing to do is to validate their fears and doubts. Technically speaking, they are not wrong in imagining the worst-case scenario, even though their outlook is limited. It's important for your child to feel validated in feeling upset, stressed, or anxious. These aren't bad emotions and therefore shouldn't be denied.

Validating your child's insecurities can also convey respect and acceptance. The purpose of listening to them isn't to fix their problems or convince them to see their experience differently; you are listening because you want to comfort them and make them feel loved despite the hurt they may be feeling inside.

A simple message like, "I understand where you're coming from. Living with ASD isn't easy. You are well within your rights to feel anxious about socializing. I get it" can be the kind of reassurance your child needs to gain the courage to confront their thoughts.

Validate Desirable Behaviors Through Positive Reinforcement

It is difficult to see your child weighed down with negativity because your natural instinct as a parent is to help them. But sometimes paying too much attention to their negative behaviors can suck you into their destructive cycle. Even though you want to be there for your child, you don't want to make it okay for them to continue the cycle of negative thinking. Ideally, you want to distract them from those harmful beliefs and encourage them to focus on uplifting thoughts.

There is another type of validation that strictly focuses on positive behaviors and ignores negative behaviors. It is known as positive reinforcement. Positive reinforcement is a technique that can help your child behave in ways that slowly improve their self-esteem. The process involves encouraging your child to repeat desirable behaviors by rewarding them whenever they perform them. The focus is on praising the good traits, attitudes, and actions that are taken, and turning a blind eye to the unwholesome traits, attitudes, and actions.

For example, when your child identifies a personal strength, you can jump on the bandwagon and show enthusiasm about their personal discovery. You might say, "That's great insight. When did you learn this about yourself?" Showing curiosity is a way of rewarding your child with attention. Long after the discussion is over, they will remember how excited you were to listen to them speak about their personal strength.

The opposite occurs when your child talks down to themselves. Since you don't want them to get into the habit of pulling themselves down, your job is to provide zero reinforcement whatsoever—not even a small amount of acknowledgement. For instance, if your child mentioned something nasty about themselves in your presence, you would pretend that you didn't hear what they said. The aim is to show no interest in the kinds of negative behaviors that you want them to change.

What makes positive reinforcement effective in adjusting your child's behaviors is the ability to choose what you pay attention to. On a subconscious level, your child learns that the best way to get your attention is to repeat desirable behaviors. Positive reinforcement can also teach you, as a parent, to switch your focus from identifying your child's mistakes to identifying moments where they behave outstandingly.

Moreover, positive reinforcement is about teaching your child to identify goodness within themselves, rather than waiting on external validation. If your child has really low self-esteem, they may not be aware of times when they are doing well and can benefit from you highlighting and praising positive behaviors.

For example, when your child sits through 30 minutes of studying, you can mention how proud you are of them. This simple gesture allows them to pause and reflect on their actions. Perhaps they didn't think that sitting through a 30-minute study session was a big deal, but now they know that it's something worth being happy about.

This example is especially important to note because it praises your child's effort, not necessarily their results. By praising your child for the small step taken toward developing healthy study habits, they feel encouraged to repeat the behavior. If you praised them only after passing the test they were studying for, it could make them feel the pressure to pass every test and be disappointed in themselves when they don't.

Offering your child gifts and other tangible rewards is not appropriate in every situation. Generally, it is best to reserve them for special occasions or big milestones in order for the gift or reward to carry significance. Remember, the purpose of positive reinforcement is to help your child improve their self-esteem, which means that whatever praise or reward you provide must be relevant to the situation and feel well-deserved.

Encourage Your Child to Dream

Some teenagers will never understand what it feels like to go through adolescence with a disability. The fact that there are certain skills, mindsets, or behaviors that don't come naturally for a young person with ASD means that they are always confronted with limitations.

Your child is perhaps used to hitting metaphoric walls and having to accept they cannot do everything "the normal way." Even when they are not rejected by their close friends and family, your child can feel rejected by society. Common social experiences that were designed to be fun and engaging for teenagers may be frustrating and unpleasant for your sensory-sensitive child.

All of this rejection and denial can make your child reluctant to grab their life with both hands and dream big. They might envision a future where they are dependent on your support and protection to get by, or one where they are confronted with one big failure after the next. Dreaming big could also be a harsh reminder of the limitations your child has to live with, which makes the exercise of visualizing the future feel stressful.

The big question is, how can you encourage your child to dream and have a positive outlook on the future? Below are some suggestions.

Create a Safe Space to Dream

Cultivate an emotionally safe environment at home that allows your child to openly share their thoughts and feelings. They might voluntarily express fears or doubts about the future and provide you with an opportunity to validate their experience and continue the conversation. Creating an emotionally safe space also means giving your child the freedom to be their own person, rather than trying to manipulate them into fitting inside a certain box.

For example, whenever your child shares visions about the future that are different from what you had in mind for them, resist the urge to debate or oppose their dream. Realize that what makes them feel alive and positive about life may not be the same as what energizes you. What's important is ensuring that your child feels comfortable sharing their unique perspectives without the fear of being judged. Whether their perspectives are similar or different to yours shouldn't be the main focus.

Model Gratitude

Another approach is to model an attitude of gratitude, openly giving thanks for what you have and recognizing the opportunities that exist in your life. Modeling this kind of attitude can have a positive impact on your child. When they notice your positive approach to life, they can feel confident in their ability to build a successful future. Gratitude teaches your child to focus on appreciating what they have instead of longing for what they don't have. This has a positive effect on your child's mind, promoting creative thinking and giving them a wider and balanced perspective of life.

Be Comfortable in Your Own Skin

Radical acceptance refers to embracing reality for what it is without attempting to change your circumstances. Practicing radical acceptance means being content with who you are and what you have, and not desiring things to be any different. Teaching your child to radically accept themselves for who they are begins with learning how to be comfortable in your own skin. When your child sees the authentic way you interact with the world, they can feel confident displaying their authentic self too.

Teach Your Child Effective Goal-Setting

Your child may have ideas about what they desire in the future, but without a clear plan and actionable steps, their ideas cannot be materialized. Whenever your child expresses a wish, challenge them to create a plan by setting goals. Goal-setting is about taking a need or desire and converting it into a specific, measurable, achievable, relevant, and time-bound plan. The process of goal-setting is designed to assess the viability of an idea and make adjustments to reduce the risk of disappointment.

Show Interest in Your Child's Passions

Your child may need reassurance to believe that their dreams are possible. One way to reassure them is to show interest in their various passions and do whatever is in your power to nurture them. Your child may have very specific fascinations that occupy their mind. These fascinations can be a window into what your child is talented in.

Without your support, they are not able to explore their fascinations deeply and develop a genuine love for their interests. Encourage your child to explore multiple fascinations without being forced to choose one. Gauge their level of interest by exposing them to different skills, knowledge, and people related to their fascination. If they are truly passionate about something, motivate them to keep exploring and never give up.

Exercise for Parents: Teach Your Teen Visualization Techniques

Your child may need support conceptualizing their goals. For instance, they may be able to write out what they would like to achieve in the coming years but struggle to imagine what that might look like in real life or the steps they need to take to get there.

Without having a mental picture of where they are heading, your child may become easily overwhelmed by the process of working toward their dream or goals. They may find it difficult to connect the hard work they are investing to the desired outcome. This is why teaching your child how to visualize the desired outcome can help them stay focused and motivated along the journey. There are three effective visualization techniques you can teach your child.

Goal Pictures

Take a photo of yourself that helps you feel inspired to achieve your goal. If possible, capture yourself performing the positive behavior you wish to adopt, holding the item you wish to purchase, or visiting the location you wish to one day travel to (since you cannot physically go there, take a photo with a symbol that reminds you of that place). Go through these photos at least once a day or a few times a week to constantly remind yourself of the end goal.

Mental Rehearsal

Close your eyes and imagine that you have achieved your goal. Mentally picture where you are, who you are with, and how you feel about yourself. What are some of the thoughts running through your mind? Now, slowly work backward and imagine the steps you had to take to reach that point, starting with the second to last step (the one right before you accomplished your goal). Spend a few minutes imagining the hardships and celebrations you experienced every step of the way. Finish your visualization by imagining the first step you have to take.

Affirmations

Create positive, present tense statements that reflect your desired outcomes. Keep your sentences simple yet meaningful so that they are easy to remember and recite in between tasks or whenever you need encouragement. Some of the ways to start your sentence include:

- "I am..."

- "I believe..."

- "I can..."

- "I feel..."

- "I deserve..."

Go through each exercise with your child and explain different scenarios where visualization can be useful, such as before an exam, when getting to know new people, or thinking about life after high school. Out of the three techniques, your child may have a favorite. Encourage them to turn this particular technique into a daily or weekly practice.

Exercise for Teens: Create a Personal Mission Statement

The best way to prepare for the future is to focus on what you want and what your journey will look like. It isn't about following the crowd and aiming for the goals that everybody else is going for. Your future will be unique because you are one of a kind!

A personal mission statement is an inspiring paragraph or essay that articulates the values that matter most to you, the goals you hope to achieve, and the ideal future you hope to see. Whenever you feel anxious about the future, you can pull out your statement and remind yourself about your priorities and the specific goals you are working toward.

To write a personal mission statement, you will need a pen and notebook. On average, this exercise will take between 15–30 minutes to complete. You can decide whether to work on this exercise alone or seek guidance from your parents.

When you are ready, answer the following questions, leaving a few lines open in between each answer.

1. Identify five core values; the qualities, attitudes, or traits that matter the most to you. For each value, give a brief explanation about why it is so important to you.

2. Identify three categories of your life that are important to building a positive future. For example, these categories could be your family, education, and health. Other categories you might mention are your social life, finances, or hobbies. For each category, create three goals that you can start working on to prepare for the future. Remember to make your goals realistic and relevant to the life you desire.

3. What positive impact do you want to make in your community, country, or the world at large? Think about how you can use what you are good at (i.e., your unique strengths and talents) to make a difference in people's lives.

On a clean sheet of paper, combine the answers that you wrote down for the three questions above to create your personal mission statement. You should have at least three paragraphs describing what you care about and the different goals you are striving toward.

Note that as you grow older, it's normal to change your mind about some of your goals. When this happens, simply update your mission statement to reflect your current values and goals.

Chapter 6:

Social Skills 101

Some of us aren't meant to belong. Some of us have to turn the world upside down and shake the hell out of it until we make our own place in it.
—Elizabeth Lowell

How Autism Spectrum Disorder Affects
Your Teen's Social Life

Social interactions are challenging for children with autism, particularly when they reach adolescence. This period is usually full of opportunities to meet new people and forge connections. Whether your child is in the classroom, playing sports, part of a social club, or networking online, there is a need for them to be able to socialize with others and display appropriate social behaviors.

Teenagers on the spectrum are fully aware of the social expectations they are presented with, such as being able to make friends, show courtesy to others, and communicate their needs effectively. Like any other young person, they desire to be included in a group and validated for who they are. They may also desire having strong bonds with friends and family members that go deeper than small talk. However, due to their inability to behave like everybody else, they are often rejected (or at least feel rejected).

There are a few ASD symptoms that make your child vulnerable to peer rejection. These may include

- an inability to interpret social cues, such as reading facial expressions and body language

- poor social skills, such as interrupting others when they are talking, making little to no eye contact during a conversation, and displaying closed off body language

- a lack of street knowledge or awareness of unspoken social rules about when and when not to bring up uncomfortable topics, how to talk with the opposite gender, and general etiquette when meeting new people or engaging in a group

- being fixed and preferring rigid rules of engagement, which make social interactions predictable, but can also make conversations feel mechanical and "uncool"

- frequently feeling anxious in social settings, which may lead to avoidant behaviors like emotionally withdrawing, defensive or aggressive behavior, or spending a lot of time alone

The naturally occurring hormonal changes in adolescence, combined with the symptoms of ASD, can make your child feel unprepared and overwhelmed by social interactions. They may feel like a fish out of water whenever stepping into new social environments that require a different set of social skills or impromptu behaviors that require flexible thinking.

In response to the increasing social pressure, it's normal for your child to have temper tantrums or lock themselves away in their bedroom, avoiding contact with family members too. The avoidant behavior can make it hard to tell what specific social challenges your child is facing and whether or not they are being bullied or harassed at school.

There are a few telltale signs that your child is experiencing social rejection or some type of emotional abuse in a different area of their life, such as school or within a friend group. Be on the lookout for the following behaviors:

- Refusal to speak about school or classmates.

- Disengagement from school work.

- Frequently complaining about headaches, stomach pain, or colds and flu.

- Becoming aggressive when they are feeling strong emotions like anger, fear, or disappointment.

- Tendency to react with emotions that are too intense for the situation.

- Tendency to zone out and appear as though they are thinking deeply about something.

- Refusal to go to school or getting into the habit of skipping certain classes.

- Pulling out of school activities or sports without a reasonable explanation.

One of the ways that your child may cope with stressful social interactions is to isolate themselves or cut off friends. At the time, this may seem like the only choice they have. The problem with self-isolating is that it removes your child from social engagements, making it difficult for them to develop social skills.

Self-isolation can also lead to the fear of social environments and the tendency to avoid contact with people who aren't close family. Once again, your child may believe this is the only way they can manage their social anxiety, but the reality is that it worsens social anxiety.

Your child may think that online interactions through social media or video games is the alternative to in-person socializing. However, since connections formed with strangers online aren't authentic, they can stunt your child's emotional development and cause them to act immature and younger than their age. They may also be naive about real-life social dynamics, such as dating, relationship boundaries, peer pressure, and so on.

Tips to Help Your Child Address Social Issues

Your child may not be outwardly crying out for help, but as a parent, you can sense when they aren't coping with social dynamics. It's important to take action as soon as you pick up on antisocial behaviors or signs of social rejection so you can help prevent your child from developing social anxiety or depression.

Nevertheless, your child is unique and may have different social needs than other children with or without ASD. Therefore, when planning your intervention, it's important to first get an understanding of where your child's mind is at, what they're feeling, and the type of support they need.

Have an open and informal conversation with your child about their social life. Ask questions about their experiences at school, engaging with teachers, interacting with classmates, or joining extracurricular activities. Allow them to lead the conversation, offering as much information as they are comfortable with.

It is also perfectly okay to express your concerns, but doing so in a compassionate and nonjudgmental way. Focus on sharing real observations that your child can also acknowledge, rather than personal opinions that come across unkind or confrontational. For example, instead of saying, "I'm worried that you are socially awkward in front of people," you can say, "I've noticed that you get quiet and find it difficult to share your thoughts when you are around people. Have you seen this too?"

Conversations that are rooted in curiosity tend to feel more open and reassuring. Your child is able to sense that your intentions aren't to change who they are, but rather to understand them better. When asking your child what support they need, lead with curiosity here too. Ask questions like, "What areas of your social life would you be comfortable with us exploring deeper?" or, "What short-term goals can we create and work on to help you become a better communicator?"

Based on their social needs, you can proceed to work on a plan to enhance their social life. Make sure that your child is leading this exercise too, since they will be the one implementing the plan. They should feel a sense of responsibility to take action and confront the fears that may be holding them back. As a parent, your role is to offer guidance and ensure that your child is staying on track to achieve their social milestones.

It's okay to offer your child suggestions on how to address their social issues, especially when they struggle to articulate what they want. For example, you might mention the following action steps.

Explore Alternatives to Traditional Social Scenes

It is possible that your child feels left out at social gatherings because they don't feel comfortable there. Perhaps they have their own ideas of a good time which don't fit the status quo. Help your child explore alternatives to traditional social scenes like house parties, sports games, or going to the movies. Encourage them to think out of the box or participate in activities related to their interests.

Find Professional Support

One of your child's needs may be to develop social skills. While this is something that you can teach them (see section below), it is better for a professional doctor to get involved. The benefit of speaking to a doctor is that they are able to understand your child in a way that you cannot. After decades of working with young people, and maybe teenagers with disabilities, they are aware of what tools and strategies to teach your child. They can also monitor your child's progress and provide helpful feedback.

Here are examples of professional doctors that can work alongside your child to improve their social experiences:

- Psychologists

- Counselors

- Psychotherapists

- Speech and language therapists

- Applied Behavioral Analysis (ABA) therapists

The benefit of taking your child to therapy is that doctors can also treat co-occurring conditions, such as anxiety, depression, low self-esteem, eating disorders, and other physical, mental health, or emotional issues your child could be living with.

Provide Opportunities to Socialize

Perhaps your child doesn't have a problem meeting people; they simply don't have enough practice with interpersonal relationships. For example, your child may be homeschooled and seldom get to interact with children their age. Or, maybe you have enforced strict social rules that prohibit your child from being exposed to different social contexts and meeting diverse people.

Loosening your reins a little bit can do wonders for your child's social life and self-esteem. Put yourself in their shoes and imagine what type of social experiences they're missing out on. How would you feel if those opportunities to network and explore the world were withheld from you?

Your very difficult (and commendable) task as a parent is to prepare your child for adulthood. This means exposing them to various experiences that can build their confidence, encourage independence, and promote resilience. If your child doesn't have much of a social life right now, work together with them to fill out their calendar. At the beginning, explore a range of social activities and situations, then gradually filter activities according to your child's interests.

The best part is that you can experience these adventures with your child, allowing you the chance to engage your inner child and have a second run at adolescence!

Social Skills Training for Teens on the Spectrum

Social skills are interactive behaviors that we use on a daily basis to communicate with each other. Developing these skills doesn't necessarily come with age (i.e., your social skills don't improve the older you get); they develop through exposure to the right information and a lot of practice!

Both teenagers with ASD and those without can find themselves lacking social skills (it is also possible for teens with autism to have exceptional social skills through years of guidance and positive reinforcement from their parents). A 2022 study conducted by the Boys & Girls Clubs of America found that 41% of adolescents 13 years and older had a difficult time accepting other people's ideas, and a third became upset when things couldn't be done their way (Boys & Girls Clubs of America, n.d.).

What this indicates is that poor social skills isn't an issue that affects teenagers on the spectrum only. It is a common problem that spreads across ages and genders. Nevertheless, for a young person with autism, not being able to communicate effectively with their peers causes added stress, on top of the existing pressure they're experiencing in different areas of their life.

Fortunately, social skills are something that you can teach and practice with your child at home. Through role playing and back and forth conversations, you can help them learn how to be a sociable person. Below are examples of skills that can improve your child's social life.

Initiating Conversations

Learning how to start a conversation can help your child build and maintain relationships. What makes this skill hard is that initiating the first contact can be intimidating!

The only way to combat the fear of starting conversations is for them to learn different conversation starters. These are greetings, comments, or questions that encourage another person to engage. Below are a few conversation starters to teach your child:

- **Asking the other person for information**: For example, in class, your child might turn to their classmate and ask, "Hey, do you know if this is a graded assignment?"

- **Paying someone a compliment**: Compliments elicit positive emotions from others. They can also be a great way to open a conversation with a stranger. For example, while standing in a group, your child might turn to someone and say, "Are those new shoes? I think they're so cool. I'd love a pair."

- **Making a general comment about a recent event everyone can relate to**: There's so much happening in the news and country that young people can talk about. From recent political updates to the latest pop song or football match, there is a lot of general information that can be used in conversations.

- **Introducing themselves formally**: It is always recommended to introduce yourself to someone you are going to be engaging with more than once. Sharing basic information like their name can be a great way for your child to start a conversation. A simple introduction would be, "Hello, my name is [name]. It's nice to meet you. What's your name?"

Keeping Conversations Going

Once your child has successfully initiated a conversation, the next step is to keep it going. Note that not every conversation is supposed to be long; sometimes your child or the other person may simply want a yes or no answer and that's all. However, genuine bonds cannot be forged with short, surface-level conversations. If they want to truly get to know someone, they will need to know how to maintain interest for a few minutes at a time.

There are a few ways your child can keep conversations interesting, such as

- **listening attentively**: Giving undivided attention to the speaker can make it easier to understand the message being shared, as well as unspoken messages such as how they may be feeling at the moment. Teach your child to maintain eye contact (or look just above the bridge of the nose) and focus on the words and tone of voice of the other person.

- **asking questions**: A great way to keep a conversation going is to show interest in the other person. This can be done by asking questions related to the message they have shared. For example, if a student makes a comment like, "I can't wait to go home!" your child might ask, "Really? Do you have anything planned for later today?"

- **looking for common ground**: Generally speaking, we enjoy talking to people who share something in common with us. You can teach your child to be mindful of similarities between them and the other person. Of course, to find these similarities, they will need to be listening attentively. It could be a shared belief, habit, feeling, or experience that both of them can resonate with. In conversation, your child might respond, "You know, I feel the same way," then proceed to unpack what they are feeling.

Understanding Sarcasm

Teenagers with ASD often find it hard to detect sarcastic speech. The reason for this is that they tend to understand information at face value. Indirect, passive, or metaphoric language can be challenging to grasp.

Sarcasm is used by witty teenagers to make light of a serious situation or make fun of another person's ignorance or behavior. For example, a student might walk past someone stuffing their face with food and comment, "You are really hungry." If the student doesn't understand sarcasm, they might respond with, "Yes, I am." However, the comment wasn't intended to be a general statement. It was a way to make light of the student's impulsive eating.

The only way to pick up on sarcasm is to be watchful of another person's nonverbal communication. Most of the time, sarcastic comments convey the opposite message of what is being acted out. There's a big mismatch between what is being said and what is being conveyed through facial expressions or gestures. Here are a few nonverbal cues that can help your child identify sarcasm:

- Exaggerated facial expressions, such as extreme rolling of the eyes, shocked face, emotionless or dull face.

- Exaggerated tone of voice, such as stretching words (e.g., you are *really* hungry), speaking with a high pitched or deep voice, sounding animated, and so on.

- A mismatch between what is being said (which generally sounds like a compliment or innocent observation) and the context of the situation (usually a very serious or uncomfortable situation). In other words, saying something that makes light of a situation that should be taken seriously.

Introspection and Taking Accountability

Another useful social skill to teach your child is how to introspect when they feel that they are being mistreated. While any young person is vulnerable to mistreatment, particularly bullying, teens with autism are at a higher risk because of their notable differences.

A 2015 meta-analysis and systematic review of 17 studies, published in the Autism Research journal, discovered that 44% of students with autism were victims of bullying, 10% were the perpetrators, and 16% were both the victims and perpetrators (Maïano et al., 2015). The most common type of bullying was verbal bullying, followed by physical bullying and relational school victimization.

Students with autism were seen to be at a higher risk of being victimized than those without autism. However, an interesting insight taken from the study is that children with ASD can be the aggressors too. Introspection can help your child reflect on an interpersonal conflict, assess what is happening, and whether their behaviors—as well as the next person's behaviors—are acceptable or unacceptable.

It's understandable why your child would react aggressively whenever they believe that someone is treating them unfairly. But before they assume the worst about the situation or individual, it is crucial for them to stop, breathe, and reflect on their own attitudes and behaviors.

Teach your child that it is common for us to misunderstand what is happening in a situation, especially when we are quick to make judgments. For example, what might seem like a teacher picking on your child could simply be their way of encouraging them to engage more in class. A simple mantra that you could repeat with your child is, "Slow to become angry, quick to listen and understand."

It's also worth reminding your child that just because they feel upset about someone's actions, doesn't mean those actions are wrong. For example, if your child is sitting too closely to one of their classmates and the student says, "Please move up, you're sitting too close to me," that shouldn't be looked upon as an offensive comment.

People are allowed to draw boundaries, which make them feel more comfortable interacting with us. We may not like or understand their boundaries, but they are not wrong or offensive either.

The same applies when a teacher is disciplining your child for talking in class or something of that nature. Your child may not appreciate being reprimanded in front of their classmates, but that doesn't make the teacher's actions wrong. Go through a few examples with your child and challenge them to answer whether the actions were fair or unfair. After every answer, explain why that particular action within that context was either fair or unfair.

Setting Firm and Clear Boundaries

After your child does some introspection and they determine that specific actions taken were unfair or abusive, they have every right to set boundaries. You can teach your child that boundaries are the invisible lines that are created between them and other people. These lines protect them from being mistreated by others.

Whenever a boundary is crossed, it is your child's responsibility to notify the boundary breaker that they have stepped over the line and their behavior is unacceptable. For example, one of your child's boundaries could be speaking with a kind tone. Whenever a student or teacher crosses the boundary by speaking with a harsh or disrespectful tone, they can raise their hand or call the person to the side and express what has happened and why it is unacceptable.

For example, your child might say to a teacher, "Ma'am, I hear what you are saying. You're right, I was making noise in class. However, I don't appreciate being spoken to in a harsh manner. Next time, could you please speak to me in a kinder tone? It will help me listen to you without feeling attacked."

What's important about this example is that your child has done some introspection and realized that the teacher's actions were correct; she was within her rights to discipline your child. Nevertheless, how the teacher chose to discipline them violated a personal boundary.

Show your child different ways to set boundaries in a respectful and compassionate way. Remind them that setting boundaries is about teaching others how to treat you, not making them feel bad or humiliated. Most of the time, students and teachers may not be aware of your child's needs or disability and can therefore act in hurtful ways without realizing the impact of their actions.

Instead of your child thinking, *This person hates me and is trying to humiliate me in front of others,* they can choose to think, *This person doesn't understand the impact of their words or actions on me. It is my job to teach them how to treat me.*

Below are a few ways of setting boundaries respectfully and compassionately. Go through these scripts with your child, practicing how to communicate the boundary appropriately:

- "It's nice to meet you. I don't like hugs, but I could give you a fist bump or high five, if you like."

- "I'm interested to hear what you have to say, but when you speak very loud, I struggle to listen. May you please lower your voice?"

- "It upsets me when you yell my name in class. I feel scared and worried. Please may you be mindful of your tone."

- "I want to attend your party, but I'm sensitive to sound. Will there be loud music there?"

- "I don't mind going out with you this weekend. However, I won't attend if [name a specific person] will be there because I don't feel comfortable around them."

Exercise for Parents: Role Play When Preparing for Difficult Conversations

Difficult conversations will come, but is your child prepared for them? Some of the instances when your child will need to engage in a difficult conversation are when they are being called in by a teacher for a performance review or bad classroom behavior, when they need to enforce a boundary with a friend, or when your child is upset with family members and seeks to express how they feel.

The best way for your child to prepare for difficult conversations is to act them out through role play, and practice different ways to approach those situations. This is an exercise that you can do together by following the steps below:

1. **Create a scenario:** The first step is to create a scenario that would call for a difficult conversation. It might be easier to start by thinking of a problem, then creating the context. For example, the problem could be your

child's bad attitude in class, a classmate's inappropriate teasing, or sibling rivalry.

2. **Add details**: Now that you have given a problem and the context of the situation, you can add details to make the story feel realistic and relevant to your child's experiences. Adding details also enables you to work with a single problem, but switch up the context of the situations. For instance, the single biggest problem your child may be dealing with is communicating their needs. By changing the details of the situation, you can help them practice expressing their needs in different contexts.

3. **Act out the scenario**: Step three may require some imagination. Your task is to act out the scenario (with you taking the role of the antagonist and your child being the protagonist). Use a simple beginning, middle, and end sequence to allow the problem to naturally unfold. Consider things like what happens right before the problem arises, during the crisis, and immediately afterward. You can also act out the "acceptable" and "unacceptable" approach to resolving the problem. This can help your child recognize their own harmful behaviors and choose to make the right choices during the heat of the moment. As the antagonist, you can also switch up your responses to help your child plan for all kinds of reactions from other people.

Exercise for Teens: More Conversation Starters

Did you enjoy going through the conversation starters mentioned above? Below are a few more scripts to help you initiate and keep conversations flowing:

1. "Could I borrow a pencil from you?"

2. "When was the last time you went to the movies?"

3. "It sounds like you really love Korean pop. What's your favorite group?"

4. "How are you feeling about the upcoming test?"

5. "This weekend is going to be sunny. Do you have any outdoor plans?"

6. "I love reading too. What's your favorite book genre?"

7. "Hey, my name is [name], but you can call me [preferred nickname] for short."

8. "You have such a cute pet. Do you mind if I pet it?"

9. "You seem cheerful today. What's on your mind?"

10. "I'm looking to start a new TV series. Do you have any recommendations?"

Chapter 7:

Navigating Friendships

You may be born into a family, but you walk into friendships. Some you'll discover you should put behind you. Others are worth every risk. —Adam Silvera

Other Factors (Besides Autism Spectrum Disorder) That Affect Your Child's Ability to Make Friends

You may be concerned that your child doesn't have a lot of friends. Perhaps, compared to their siblings or your own upbringing, your child seems to have a dull social life. At the back of your mind, you fear that they could be depressed or hiding something critical, like being a victim of bullying.

But in reality, that may not be the case at all. Yes, it's true that being diagnosed with ASD makes the process of building and maintaining relationships challenging, but it certainly isn't impossible. There are some teens on the spectrum who have no trouble making friends and engaging in different social environments, but then there are some who hide away from people and avoid or feel overwhelmed by connections.

Your child will possibly fall somewhere in between those two extremes. However, there could also be other factors affecting their ability to make friends. These include

1. **social anxiety**: Your child may be battling with social anxiety, a condition that makes them fearful of embarrassing themselves in public. This makes it difficult for them to get out of their own thoughts, interact with others, or initiate conversations.

2. **adjusting to a recent move**: If your child has recently changed schools, or your family has recently relocated to a new city, it's normal for them to drag their feet in making friends. They could be processing the separation from their previous friend group and

doubtful that they will receive the same warmth and support again. Getting to know new people can also be a daunting exercise, especially for teens who are self-conscious.

3. **difficulty trusting others**: Your child may have been abused or bullied by school children in the past, which has caused them to lose trust in friendships. To prevent themselves from being hurt again, they might put up high walls and make it difficult for other people to get to know them.

4. **introversion**: Introverted teenagers (with or without ASD) have a laid-back approach when it comes to making friends. Since they are naturally shy, it's hard for them to initiate conversations, follow up with friends, or take advantage of opportunities to build friendships, such as joining a sports team or school club.

5. **lack of self-awareness**: Self-awareness is an emotional intelligence skill that helps children understand their own thoughts, emotions, and behaviors, particularly why they act, feel, or think a certain way. The lack of self-awareness means that your child is unable to reflect on the way they approach other people. For example, they wouldn't be able to tell when their words or actions negatively affect someone. The lack of self-awareness could be a reason why a child may find it easy to make friends, but difficult to keep them.

How to Gently Nudge Your Child to Make Friends

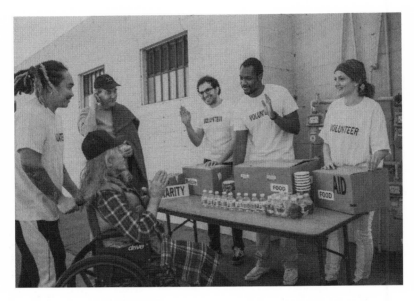

Before you take over your child's social calendar, realize the fact that not every teenager will have the same teenage experience. Even among your children, each person will have their own unique experience of adolescence. Some of your kids might have a buzzing social life, while others will have only one or two friends and prefer staying at home on weekends.

If your child is introverted by nature and doesn't really care about making friends, accept them for who they are. Find ways to accommodate their minimal social needs, even if it means that you become one of their few friends!

On the other hand, if your child expresses a desire to make friends, despite being held back by fear or trust issues, you can take the lead and show them different ways to meet new people. Below are a few suggestions to propose.

Joining Clubs, Teams, and Committees

Your child has a better chance of making a good first impression when they are feeling confident. What better way to raise your child's confidence than encouraging them to join an interest-based group? Being able to speak openly about a subject or activity they care about can make starting conversations and finding commonalities with others easier!

Volunteering

Your child may have a soft spot for people, animals, or the environment. Volunteering is another type of interest-based activity that allows your child to network with younger and older people while working together toward a common goal. This sense of comradery can make your child feel safe and accepted. Plus, they get to build a family outside of their traditional family: the family that they choose!

Finding a Part-Time Job

Making friends is all about exposing yourself to different people and places. You never truly know who would be a lifelong friend without venturing outside of your comfort zone. Encourage your child to make friends by applying for a part-time job at a local coffee shop, retail store, or activity center. The best time to do this would be during summer vacation, where other teens are likely to be looking for part-time work too.

Support Groups and Forums

Your child may feel less anxious getting to know other teenagers who are on the spectrum. The common challenges and opportunities they share can be what unites them. In-person support groups are preferred over virtual support groups or forums due to being safer and more socially rewarding. However, in the absence of physical groups, your child can search for verified virtual groups and forums.

Signs Your Teen Has a Toxic Friend and What You Can Do About It

Not every friendship your child forms will be healthy. In their excitement to get to know people or fit into a group, your child could run into someone who is abusive or manipulative. A toxic friend never comes across that way, at least in the beginning. They are able to blindside your child until it becomes difficult to separate them.

As an adult, you have run into strange characters in your personal and professional life and know how charming toxic people can be when they are still baiting their victims. Your child doesn't have as much experience as you to tell when an individual is acting too good to be true. They may even lack the proper boundaries to enforce a safe distance between themselves and others, thereby attracting toxic friends who demand all of their time, energy, and devotion.

The first thing to do when you sense that your child is friends with someone toxic is to study their friendship. It may be useful to keep a record of recurring patterns of behavior that are alarming. This will give you factual information to base your assumptions on. A few behavioral patterns to look out for include

1. **nasty comments disguised as jokes**: There's a difference between innocent joking and nasty joking. In general, for a joke to be funny, it shouldn't be made at the expense of someone else. If your child's friend is making hurtful jokes that cause your child to doubt themselves, they are displaying typical passive-aggressive behavior.

2. **subtle acts of sabotage**: Another pattern that is a red flag in friendships is carrying out subtle acts of sabotage. For instance, arriving an hour late to a meetup, pulling out of a plan at the last minute, spreading unfounded rumors behind your child's back, or undermining your child in the presence of other people are all examples of subtle acts of sabotage. When you observe these behaviors closely, they are unkind and not something that a respectful person would do.

3. **imbalance of power**: Is your child always giving to a friend who doesn't return their kind gestures? If so, the friendship could be one-sided. Reciprocation is the bedrock of healthy relationships, and without it, one person is bound to invest more time and effort than the other. If your child is doing most of the giving, they are vulnerable to being taken for granted or manipulated into serving the needs of the other person.

4. **inconsistency**: It's normal for friendships to start out slow and steady. This is the natural way that strangers grow to become acquaintances, then good friends. If you notice that your child is in a hot and cold friendship, where one week they are spending a lot of time with their friend and the next week they can't get a hold of them, this is a red flag. Inconsistency is a sign of a lack of emotional availability. Overtime, your child may get hurt forming a connection with someone who is avoidant or dismissive of them.

If you have noted these and other examples of toxic behavior, you can approach your child with factual evidence. But before you do, make sure that you process any built up resentment toward your child's friend. Ideally, you want the conversation to be constructive, not charged with emotion.

At most, you are seeking to caution your child about this particular friend without sharing your personal opinion. Unless you suspect the friend to be dangerous (e.g., someone who is negatively changing your child's behaviors, such as introducing them to destructive behaviors), you cannot force your child to break ties with them.

With that being said, you can share your observations about the worrying behaviors. However, as much as possible, focus on bringing attention to the toxic behavior instead of the toxic friend. Bring out the notes you have been taking for a while and let your child know what behaviors you find worrying.

For example, you might say, "I've noticed that you always travel to see your friend and she hasn't traveled to see you. It looks to me like the friendship could be one-sided, where you're doing most of the work and your friend isn't helping you."

After making your observations known, you can reassure your child that this isn't an attack on their friend. But since you are protective of them, it's important to share concerns you may have about their friendship. If your child dismisses your observations, let the conversation go. Trust that they have made a note of what you said and will remember your words at a later stage.

Another approach you can take is tightening your structure at home to prevent regular interactions with the same toxic friend. For example, if your child has a close friend who is introducing them to destructive habits, you can enforce new rules around going out at night, visiting the homes of friends, or sleeping over at friends 'houses.

Your new rules shouldn't prevent your child from engaging in these experiences, but enforce stricter limits. For example, your child may be permitted to sleep over at a select group of people's houses, and you must first get to know their parents before that can happen. Or, they may be permitted to go to a house party, but they're not allowed to take any substances like drugs, cigarettes, or alcohol.

Exercise for Parents: Prepare for New Friends That Enter Your Child's Life

The older your child gets, the more independence they demand. Most times, this means that you are not given as much say about who they can or can't be friends with. But, since you are still their parent and have the responsibility to protect them, you have a right to oversee their social life. Below are a few ways to prepare for meeting new friends:

- **Build a solid relationship with your child**: The first and most important tip is to strengthen the relationship with your child. When you know them from back to front, you can easily pick up on subtle changes in their behaviors. They may even voluntarily share information about their friends and show willingness to take your advice.

- **Get to know their friends**: Create opportunities to meet and spend time with your child's friends. Perhaps you can host a lunch or game night at your house and ask your child to invite their friends. Casually get to know them and ask questions about school, family, and hobbies. This shouldn't feel like an interview, otherwise they may not feel comfortable opening up about themselves.

- **Get to know the parents**: If possible, schedule coffee with your child's friends 'parents, or take advantage of opportunities to meet them at school. You can learn a lot about a child by observing their parents. When engaging with the parents, get a sense of who they are, how much time they spend with their kid, what they value or believe, and what type of family dynamic they have at home.

Exercise for Teens: Checklist—Are You a Good Friend?

As you step out of your shell and start making friends, you'll need to work on adopting the traits of a good friend so you are able to make your friends feel safe and supported.

Here is a checklist of common traits you will find in a good friend. You can use this checklist in two ways: To determine whether the new person you are getting to know has the qualities of a good friend, or when reflecting on how much of a good friend you are to others and which traits you still need to work on.

Questions	Yes	No
Do you know the difference between right and wrong?		
Do you speak out against injustice, unfair treatment, or bullying?		
Do you tell the truth, even if doing so may get you in trouble?		
Do your words match your behaviors?		
Do you keep your promises/avoid making promises that you can't keep?		

Questions	Yes	No
Can other people depend on you to be on time?		
Do you make yourself available when your friends are going through a difficult time?		
Do you avoid speaking negatively about your friends in their absence?		
Do you defend your friends when other people talk badly about them?		
Are you able to give your friends good advice when they need it?		
Are you able to stand up to your friends when they have crossed a boundary?		
Do you feel comfortable disagreeing with your friend without feeling like you are hurting their feelings?		
Do you show respect to your friends, even when they have different opinions?		
Are you capable of having deep conversations with your friends about general topics?		
Are you able to have light and entertaining conversations?		

Questions	Yes	No
Do you know details about your friends' aspirations in life, like what they hope to do after high school?		
Do you allow your friend to be themselves and make whatever decisions they choose?		
Are you capable of celebrating your friends' achievements without feeling intimidated?		
Do you find it easy to respect your friends' boundaries?		
Are you comfortable spending time alone as much as you do with your friends?		

Chapter 8:

Techniques to Avoid Power

Struggles and Negotiate Rules

*Trying to win a power struggle is like trying to win a nuclear war. You may achieve your goal, but not without catastrophic casualties on both sides. –*Jamie Raser

What Are Power Struggles?

A *power struggle* can be defined as "a subtle or visible battle for power and control in a relationship." In most cases, the individual seeking more power feels disempowered and desires to correct the perceived imbalance. Other times, a power struggle comes after years of someone being complicit to another person's overbearing behavior, where they finally reach their breaking point.

What makes a power struggle chaotic is the manner in which control is demanded. The disempowered individual will not respectfully express their needs or set boundaries; they will viciously grab whatever power they can and use different kinds of aggressive and avoidant behaviors to signal their disapproval.

It's worth mentioning that a power struggle isn't the same as butting heads with a loved one. Disagreements are natural and expected in all types of relationships due to the different needs and personality traits of individuals.

A power struggle is more serious than a disagreement. The aim is not to come together and cooperate on a way forward; rather, it's to demand rights and privileges without negotiation. It is the deliberate refusal to participate in any kind of conflict resolution or problem-solving to reach a mutual understanding.

When you are in a power struggle, you can feel like you have reached a dead end in the relationship. The way forward isn't clear because the core issues aren't discussed and resolved in an appropriate manner. Obliging to the demands made by the other person may seem like a quick solution; however, it doesn't bring an end to the power struggle. In fact, once the other person realizes that they can get their way without compromising or resolving issues, they tend to demand even more power.

How Power Struggles Manifest in Parent-Child Relationships

A study on heterosexual couples, conducted in 2021, found that power differences (i.e., one partner having slightly more power than the other) didn't negatively affect the relationship dynamic. However, how each person understood and interpreted the difference in their level of power influenced the health of the relationship (Körner & Schütz, 2021).

What this shows is that one's perception of their level of power determines how safe and secure they feel in the relationship, even if they don't hold most of the power in the relationship. As long as they feel empowered, such as feeling respected and validated by the other person, they will experience high relationship satisfaction.

We know that teenagers have less power in the parent-child relationship, but this isn't what causes a power struggle. Teenagers who enter power struggles have, for a certain period, felt disempowered in the relationship. Perhaps they aren't being heard or validated the way they desire, or given the freedom, privacy, or respect they're asking for.

Eventually, they reach a point where they become frustrated with constantly having to ask for the same needs without being met with openness and understanding. The only way they believe that change will occur in their parent-child relationship is to take power by force. Below are examples of behaviors that disgruntled teenagers may display when they are engaging in power struggles:

- Refusal to see where you are coming from, even if you are making valid points backed with evidence.

- Reluctance to compromise or work together to find solutions.

- Engaging in controlling behavior, such as wanting to have the last word, changing the rules to accommodate their desires, and making demands rather than requests.

- Using manipulation tactics to influence parent's behaviors. These may include lying, gaslighting, faking tears, having a temper tantrum, or giving ultimatums.

- Refusal to accept and abide by the rules or show respect for other people's boundaries.

- Holding grudges and punishing parents with passive-aggressive behavior (i.e., silent treatment) to convey disapproval.

- Giving up easily when resolving conflict; tendency to walk out of a discussion or refuse to listen to the other person.

- Engaging in acts of sabotage, especially when they are asked to complete a task.

Being involved in a power struggle with your teenager can be demoralizing. It can seem like whatever you do to accommodate your child doesn't work. No amount of pleading, bending the rules, or showing compassion makes them cooperate with you.

The commitment you will need to make when seeking to end— or maybe prevent—a power struggle is to empathize with your child. Showing empathy is about parking your own thoughts and emotions and stepping inside your child's world. This may be difficult to do if you are still feeling deeply hurt by your child, thus it is recommended to start with understanding how you feel and talking through your issues with your spouse or a therapist.

The truth of the matter is that the power struggle is equally as exhausting and emotionally draining for your child as it is for you. It pains them to continue the battle for power and defy all logic with their chaotic behaviors. Ideally, your child desires to restore harmony in your relationship, but there are certain changes that need to be made.

Why Making Threats Doesn't Work With Teens on the Spectrum

In your frustration, you might yell and make threats to your child, believing that confronting their aggression with your aggression will do the trick. After all, you're the parent and they should eventually back down, right? Well, that's not exactly how it works with teenagers on the spectrum.

Children with autism often experience some degree of language processing challenges. This means that they are less reactive to threatening language. It also means that you may need to repeat instructions over and over again before they remember to do what's right.

Yelling and making threats to a child with language processing challenges is ineffective because listening doesn't come easy for them. Furthermore, they may not be able to connect your loud voice or tense face with the gravity of their inappropriate behavior. They are more likely to think that raising your voice is an acceptable way of expressing anger, and before you know it, they have adopted the same aggressive behavior when feeling upset.

On a personal level, making threats to your child can negatively impact the relationship between you. Here are some of the side effects of displaying this kind of behavior when seeking to end a power struggle:

1. **Threats instill fear**: Threatening your child whenever they seek to assert control causes them to become fearful of you. While this may seem to prevent power struggles in the short-term, it leads to an erosion of trust and a potential breakdown of your relationship later in life.

2. **Threats make your child feel disempowered**: When you make threats, your child's needs go unaddressed, making them feel powerless in the relationship. They may not be strong enough to challenge you any further without significantly hurting themselves, so they walk away from the interaction feeling defeated and misunderstood.

3. **Threats don't create a teaching opportunity**: If you are prone to making threats to your child, they miss out on plenty of teachable moments where you can explain the reasons why their behavior is inappropriate. The message ingrained in their mind is, If I do what my parents say, I will avoid punishment. Their core motivation is to avoid punishment, rather than improving their character and developing good habits.

If your child is displaying aggressive behavior, showing more aggression doesn't help to correct their behavior. It only teaches them that responding to situations with aggression is acceptable. The best way to end or prevent a power struggle is to avoid getting roped into the battle for power in the first place.

As the parental figure in your child's life, you hold the highest authority. This isn't something that you need to prove whenever you are provoked or challenged. Instead, you can show how much power you have by choosing to manage the situation in a positive and nonthreatening way while still maintaining boundaries and consequences.

Techniques to Avoid Power Struggles

Being secure in your role as a parent can help you avoid entering power struggles with your child. It's important to be confident in who you are and how you have chosen to parent your child so that you have clear limits about what you can and cannot accept.

For example, we know that with age, teenagers will make demands for more independence. But how much independence they get to enjoy is completely up to you. The decision for setting healthy limits shouldn't be left to your child, or any other person for that matter.

Nevertheless, with this much power comes the responsibility to be fair and empathetic toward your child's needs. They already know that they can't override your rules, so make sure that you're considering your child's adolescent needs in every decision you make.

Below are some techniques for avoiding power struggles and getting your child to willingly cooperate with you.

Discourage Defiant Behavior

One of the first things to establish with your child is that without open and honest communication, nobody will walk away feeling heard and validated. Their defiant behavior will not help them convey the messages they want to. If anything, it will make you completely shut off to them (refer back to the section on positive reinforcement).

Point out the disadvantages of them continuing to behave this way while simultaneously encouraging them to calm down and open up to you. For example, you can say, "Listen buddy, I can tell you're upset. However, I can't engage with you when you are like this, I need you to be willing to cooperate with me. I can see that you're upset with me and I want to understand why."

Identify What Your Child Needs

Remember this: Your child wouldn't be engaging in a power struggle if they felt empowered in the relationship. There must be a recent situation or series of events that have taken place which have led to them revolting against your leadership. Once again, switch on your empathy and get down to their level. Try to understand their underlying needs that have gone unrecognized or been disregarded.

For this exercise, take out a notebook and journal about recent developments in your parent-child relationship. Note the ways that both you and your child have changed over the past months or years. Write down the recurring issues you have been experiencing in your relationship and resolutions (if any) that you have been able to come up with.

The aim is to identify areas of contention and possible needs that your child has that have gone unnoticed or unaddressed.

Bear in mind that what they need may not be something you consider a priority or even appropriate. However, you don't need to be in agreement with your child to validate their needs.

Be Willing to Compromise

For as long as your child has needs that are not being fulfilled, they will hold resentment or seek control by force. Their built up rage can also negatively impact their concentration at school, relationships with friends, or overall motivation for life. Therefore, even if you don't fully agree with your child's needs, you must open the discussion and be willing to make compromises.

Before having a conversation with your child, write down your absolute nonnegotiables; those ideas or actions which you cannot accept no matter what. Walk into the conversation with your list of nonnegotiables. Lay them out early so that your child understands the parameters for negotiations.

Thereafter, do more listening and asking of questions than talking to understand what your child truly needs and how you can bend the rules to provide it for them.

Provide Two Great Choices

If you'd like to avoid reaching the stage of negotiations, offer your child two great choices. Both choices should address your child's needs, even if they're not what they had in mind. For example, your child may need more privacy at home and demand a key for their bedroom door.

Purchasing a key may not be an option for you because of your no-lock policy at home. So, instead, you give them two great choices:

- **Choice 1**: Creating a "Do not disturb" sign and hanging it outside their door whenever they want to be left alone.

- **Choice 2**: Introducing a quiet hour every day where the entire family retreats to their own corners in the house and spends time alone.

When given two choices, your child is encouraged to pick one. You can decide if you are open to making compromises or not. In the event that your child refuses to make a choice, or shuts down both choices, let them know that you are not willing to discuss their need for privacy until they cooperate with you. You might say, "I have listened to what you need and want to make that possible for you. But if you refuse to work with me, there is nothing more I can do."

Hold Your Child Accountable

After both of you have successfully negotiated new rules of engagement, draft a memorandum of understanding (MOU). This is a one or two page document, signed by all parties, that states what has been agreed upon and possible consequences for violating the agreement.

Discuss with your child what would be fair consequences for them not following the new rules. It's important that they help to set the consequences to avoid future power struggles in the event of breaking the rules. Your MOU can also include a trial period of 7 or 30 days where your child familiarizes themselves with the new expectations before formally committing to them.

During the trial period, breaking rules will not count against your child, since they are technically still learning the new behavior. However, it may cause both of you to go back to the drawing board and readjust the rules once the period is over.

Exercise for Parents: Practice Scripts for Effective Negotiations

It's common for teenagers to feel dissatisfied with their parents 'rules. They may have formed their own ideas and believe there are better ways of enforcing house rules or boundaries. Listening to your child and leaving room for negations can help them feel empowered in your parent-child relationship.

Negotiations are not an overthrow of your current rules, but more of a modification that accommodates your child's evolving needs. Below are a few tips on what to say during a negotiation to maintain control of the conversation and create win-win outcomes:

- **Convey a willingness to listen:** Open the conversation by giving your child the opportunity to share what's on their mind. Let them know that you are willing to listen without judgment.

  - Script: "Thank you for sitting down with me. I just wanted to know how you're doing and what's on your mind. I'm willing to give you my full attention and hear what you have to say."

- **Acknowledge the legitimacy of their perspective:** As your child speaks, they will make some valid points. Nod your head, smile, and say words like, "That's true" or "Yes, I agree with you on that." Doing this shows your child that you are flexible and empathetic to their needs.

  - Script: "You have made some really good points. I liked what you said about [quote two or three points mentioned]."

- **Choose your battles wisely:** If the issue isn't one that you consider serious, go along with your child's suggestion and let them have their way. Conserve your time and energy for bigger issues that go against your values or fall outside your established limits. Have the courage to back down and support your child in whatever they need. It is also perfectly fine to say, "You know what, you're right! I change my mind."

  - Script: "I have listened to what you have to say and I can't find any reason to oppose your request. I'm willing to give you what you need. Please explain in detail how I can support you."

- **Raise your concerns and brainstorm ideas**: You may not entirely be opposed to your child's idea, but have a few concerns about agreeing to their plan. Present the concerns you have and ask your child to suggest solutions. It may help to write the solutions down on paper and go through a process of elimination until you have one that incorporates both of your needs.

  - Script: "I hear what you're saying. However, I have a few concerns about this request, such as [list your concerns]. What solutions might you suggest to address these concerns?"

Exercise for Teens: Confident Ways to Present an Argument to Your Parents

Presenting an argument and "arguing" are not the same thing. When you present an argument, you offer a different perspective in hopes of winning the other person over. Arguing, on the other hand, is about fighting to be right or come out on top.

Whenever you are feeling upset with your parents, it's usually better to present an argument (instead of arguing) and help them see where you're coming from. Below are some useful tips for presenting an argument in a confident way.

Step One: Think About What You Need

Before approaching your parents, spend time thinking about what you need from them. Do you want to make a request for support? An adjustment of rules? Permission to go somewhere? Write your need down on a piece of paper, starting with the words, "I need," and give yourself a day to look over the need and make a few changes, if necessary.

Here are a few examples of needs:

- "I need your permission to go out at night with my friends."

- "I need support organizing my school work and coming up with a timetable."

- "I need to bring up an issue I have with the way you talk to me."

Step Two: Explain the Emotional Impact

When presenting your argument, it's always good to mention how you are affected by the way things are currently. In other words, you will need to describe how not having your needs met makes you feel. Once again, it might be easier to reflect and take notes about how you are feeling before approaching your parents.

Here are a few ways to describe the emotional impact:

- "I feel scared to speak to you about this because I don't know how you will react."

- "I'm worried that if I don't get support soon, my school performance will continue to plunge."

- "I feel belittled when you speak down to me."

Step Three: Show Willingness to Compromise

After you have stated what you need and how it makes you feel, finish off by reassuring your parents that you are willing to hear what they have to say and meet somewhere in the middle. Remember that compromise doesn't mean you have lost all hopes of getting what you want. It simply means that you are open to finding ways of making sure both you and your parents are happy with the new expectations.

Here are some examples of conveying your willingness to compromise:

- "I know that you may have some concerns. I'm willing to listen and see how we can meet in the middle."

- "Now that you know how I feel, I'm open to listening to how you feel."

- "What I'm asking for may be unexpected, but I think we can find a way to make it work for both of us."

Rehearse these three steps before presenting arguments to your parents. Let your focus be on speaking from the heart and giving your parents a sneak peak into your world. Be prepared to make compromises that slightly differ from what you had in mind, but still respond to what you need!

Chapter 9:

How to Lead From Behind and

Help Your Teen Become an

Independent Young Person

Parents are the ultimate role models for children. Every word, every movement, and action affects. No other person or outside force has a greater influence on a child than a parent. –Bob Keeshan

What Does It Mean to Lead From Behind?

Leading from behind is a style of leadership used in the corporate world. The team leader transfers decision-making power to their employees, allowing them to take charge of their work tasks and goals.

A good analogy to describe leading from behind is looking at how shepherds lead their flock of sheep. Shepherds are always at the back, overseeing the movements of the flock and making sure that none are lost along the way. By leading from behind, shepherds also enable the faster and more agile sheep to take the reins and walk in front of the flock, setting the pace for the rest of the sheep to follow.

Likewise, some leaders in the corporate world know that the only way to get the best from their teams is to take a step back and provide enough freedom and decision-making power for employees to give their best work. Being too involved in every process can stunt creativity and reduce team morale.

There are a lot of risks associated with transferring more power and ownership of work to employees. For instance, what happens when the leader steps back and the team's performance drops? In order to make this type of leadership style effective, a lot of planning is involved.

For example, the leader must develop a strong foundation of trust and ensure that all employees understand their team roles and responsibilities. They should also share a common vision that is clear and specific enough for their employees to follow and draw inspiration from.

It is also expected for leaders to be available whenever the team needs support and guidance. Sharing expert advice, without necessarily taking on the team's problems, can be the kind of motivation employees need to soldier on.

How to Lead From Behind as a Parent

Leading from behind can be a great parenting approach to use with your child. In a practical sense, it would involve taking a step back and giving your child permission to make their own decisions and solve their own problems. The only time you would step in is to provide solicited feedback and support, or caution your child when you believe they're going down the wrong path.

Making this adjustment may not be easy for you, especially if you have spent close to two decades leading from the front and setting the pace and goals for your child. Taking a step back could make you feel unimportant in your child's life. But the truth is that leading from behind doesn't make your role as a parent any less important. It simply gives you a different purpose in your child's life.

Over the adolescent years, as your child demands more and more independence, your purpose in their life shifts from the nurturer to the mentor. The love between you is still the same; however, the need for you changes in your child's life. The good news is that as your teenager enters adulthood, their need for a mentor becomes increasingly significant, and you will find them reaching out to you as they make important career, finance, and relationship decisions.

If you would like to practice leading from behind, below are a few suggestions that you can follow.

Ask Questions Rather Than Make Demands

Avoid the temptation to direct your child's behavior. In a few years, they will be thrust into adulthood and expected to direct their own life. Instead of telling your teen what to do, ask questions to train them to be mindful of their own wants and needs and think deeply about the effects of their behaviors.

For example, if you are aware that an assignment deadline is approaching and your child hasn't completed the work, avoid coaching them on how and when to get the work done. Instead, ask questions like:

- "When is your assignment due?"

- "What's the scope of the assignment?"

- "How many more days do you have left to complete the task?"

- "What will happen if you don't submit the assignment on time?"

These questions allow your child to assess the situation and get an idea of what's expected of them. Whether they choose to do the work or not is their prerogative, but at least they're fully aware of the consequences of not submitting on time.

Set Parameters, but Create Enough Room for Exploration

Leading from behind doesn't mean doing away with rules and expectations for your child; however, you shouldn't be too overly controlling of how they choose to apply the rules. For example, your child may not make their bed as you would like them to, but be proud of the fact that they have made their bed!

Remember that your child is their own person and has their own metrics and standards. What works for them may not work for you, but that isn't what you should focus on. Allow them to express their individuality, even when it comes to meeting your expectations. As long as they follow your rules, it shouldn't matter how they carry them out.

Express Faith in Your Child's Ability to Solve Problems

Whenever your child is in a crisis, express how much faith you have in them finding a solution. Offer advice that is both practical and encouraging, then take a step back and refocus on your own tasks. As your parenting role shifts from nurturer to mentor, you will need to step back often and allow your child the privilege to fail and learn from their mistakes, or perhaps repeat the same mistake over and over again and learn through natural consequences.

Expressing faith in your child is as simple as validating what they are going through and reassuring them that they have the strength to overcome it. For instance, you might say, "It sounds like you're going through a tough time, and I sincerely believe that you will make the right decision. I trust you to find the best solution."

Sometimes your child may not be open to taking advice, so make sure you ask before you share your opinion.

Different Ways to Foster Independence

Even though teenagers crave a lot of freedom and independence, they usually don't have the skills and knowledge to manage having that much responsibility in their lives. Moreover, they may be ignorant of the kind of character development needed to become an independent and responsible individual.

An important life lesson to teach your child is that nothing in life comes easy. Not only do they need to work for the life of their dreams, but they're also responsible for adjusting their mindset and habits to match the kind of career, health, and relationships they desire.

With freedom comes great responsibility and sometimes pressure. Since it is your desire to raise a successful young person, you have the important task of teaching your child the necessary skills to become independent. This means allowing them enough room to take on more adult responsibilities while monitoring their progress and offering guidance along the way.

Below are some of the practical ways to foster independence in your child:

- Let your child choose household chores and preferred chore schedules.

- Present opportunities for your child to network with adults, such as allowing them to shadow you at work, or inviting them as your plus one at a work or social function.

- Encourage your child to earn their monthly allowance by running errands for the family, washing the family car, walking the pets, or helping you with personal tasks.

- Expose your child to the workforce before they graduate from high school. Take them through the process of creating a résumé, applying for summer jobs, and practicing professional etiquette for interviews.

- Allow your child to practice their driving skills by giving them the car on the weekends. You are welcome to set parameters, like the distance they are allowed to go and when they should be back home. You can also add a disclaimer, such as expecting them to refill the gas after taking the car for a spin.

- If you have an older teenager who has graduated from high school and is working, set an expectation for them to contribute a small portion of their wages toward household expenses. This becomes their "rent" for living at home.

- Encourage your child to draft a career development plan, and use your professional experience to help them refine goals and focus on specific action steps. Meet with them every quarter to assess progress and make adjustments to the plan.

- Teach your child important life skills to manage emergencies or take care of themselves in your absence. These might include skills like how to change a tire, put out a fire at home, protect themselves during house break-ins, or what to do when the power is out or when they get into an accident on the road.

Exercise for Parents: How to Recognize Teachable Moments

As teens get older, parents need to get smarter about how they deliver important life messages without sounding too preachy or controlling.

Capitalizing on teachable moments helps parents make a connection between behavior and outcomes as a situation unfolds naturally. The advice given sounds genuine and relevant to what is happening at the moment.

It's difficult to predict a teachable moment because they are spontaneous and unplanned. However, you can train yourself to be on the lookout for these golden opportunities to impart wisdom to your child.

Here are some tips on how to recognize teachable moments:

- **When your child asks a question, seeking more than a yes or no answer**: For example, they might ask, "Can I become successful without going to college?" Your response could be, "Yes, of course you can. Success doesn't require a college degree. It requires a clear vision and plenty of hard work."

- **When you are watching TV or listening to music**: For example, while driving your child to school, there might be a song playing on the radio that has powerful lyrics that you can highlight. Or, during a series binge, there might be a scene that depicts a real-life crisis that relates to your child, which you can discuss together.

- **After your child has made a mistake**: When correcting your child's behavior, encourage a moment of reflection about what they can do better next time. Draw a connection between their actions and the unpleasant outcome, and brainstorm alternative actions they could have taken.

Exercise for Teens: Habits of Independent Young People

With independence comes responsibility to act with more integrity and live a productive lifestyle. There are common habits that independent people develop, which help them build and maintain positive attitudes and behaviors.

Below are examples of the kinds of behaviors that can help you develop independence. Challenge yourself to work toward adopting these behaviors, starting with one behavior at a time.

1. **Independent people set goals and work diligently on them**: Create a short-term goal (i.e., a goal you can achieve within six months) in any area of your life, and set daily, weekly, and monthly action steps to help you accomplish it.

2. **Independent people take responsibility for their actions (good or bad)**: Practice reflecting on your actions in a journal, noting what you did well and where you can improve next time. Avoid blaming others, judging yourself, or making excuses about why things turned out the way they did.

3. **Independent people are self-motivated**: Become your biggest cheerleader by encouraging yourself several times a day to continue being a rock star! Create positive affirmation cards, a vision board, or a jar of gratitude (filling a mason jar with notes about your small wins). When you are upset or disappointed, have different soothing activities to relieve stress and uplift your mood.

4. **Independent people make decisions on their own**: The next time you're expected to make a decision, spend 15–30 minutes collecting information on the internet or consulting your parents. Summarize the information and identify at least two options that you can take (you are welcome to identify more options).

Weigh the pros and cons of each option, then see which one is the most favorable. The final step is the hardest: Believe in yourself enough to take action and follow through with your decision. If you make a mistake or achieve undesirable results, look for ways to improve next time.

Conclusion

Parents need to fill a child's bucket of self-esteem so high that the rest of the world can't poke enough holes to drain it dry. —Alvin Price

The transition from adolescence to adulthood won't always be smooth-sailing. Some teenagers can have a difficult time adjusting to the changes in their bodies, as well as the increased pressure and responsibilities at home and at school. This is also the period where teens are finding their voice, developing a separate identity from their parents, and becoming their own person, which means more questioning of rules and struggles for power and independence.

As a parent raising a young person on the spectrum, you can at times wonder whether their behaviors are symptoms of their disorder or normal stages of adolescence. The truth is that ASD doesn't become worse during adolescence; it simply makes the normal challenges teenagers face tougher to manage.

This means that the changes in your child's attitudes and behaviors are due to typical social and behavioral changes experienced during puberty; however, being diagnosed with a cognitive and developmental disorder makes these changes significantly more stressful. It's normal and expected for teens to be stubborn, tell lies, or act out when they don't get their way. But if you're concerned that your child's defiant behaviors could be symptoms of something else, such as ODD, consider seeking medical attention.

To safely make it through this six-year transition, both you and your child will need to make adjustments in order for your relationship to continue blooming during this period of life. For example, you may need to know when to step back, listen rather than speak, and provide positive reinforcement instead of criticism. Your child, on the other hand, will need to learn how to identify and express their emotions, self-soothe whenever they feel overwhelmed, improve their organizational skills, know when to negotiate and when to simply follow the rules, and take responsibility for their actions.

Fortunately, this book includes 18 exercises for you and your child to practice so that you can both learn how to compromise, listen and respond to each others 'needs, and strive to create win-win situations that deepen your parent-child bond!

Being diagnosed with ASD doesn't need to hinder your child from becoming a confident, independent, and ambitious young person. The unique challenges they face can be overcome with self-awareness and a toolbox of psychological skills that help to manage autism symptoms. It's important for your child to continue visualizing a better future and working on achieving the goals they set out, one step at a time. With the right mindset and attitude, nothing is impossible for them!

If you have found this book valuable in parenting your teenager with autism, kindly leave a review on the book's Amazon page.

About the Author

Richard Bass is a well-established author with extensive knowledge and background on children's disabilities. Richard has also experienced first-hand many children and teens who deal with depression and anxiety. He enjoys researching techniques and ideas to better serve students, as well as providing guidance to parents on how to understand and lead their children to success.

Richard wants to share his experience, research, and practices through his writing, as it has proven successful to many parents and students. He feels there is a need for parents and others around the child to fully understand the disability, or the mental health of the child. He hopes that with his writing, people will be more understanding of children going through these issues.

Richard Bass has been in education for over a decade and holds a bachelor's and master's degree in education as well as several certifications, including Special Education K-12 and Educational Administration. Whenever Richard is not working, reading, or writing, he likes to travel with his family to learn about different cultures, as well as get ideas from all around the world about the upbringing of children, especially those with disabilities. He also researches and learns about different international educational systems.

Richard participates in several online groups where parents, educators, doctors, and psychologists share their success with children with disabilities. He is in the process of growing a Facebook (Meta) group where further discussion about his books and techniques could take place. Apart from online groups, he has also attended training regarding the upbringing of students with disabilities and has also led training in this area.

A Message from the Author

If you enjoyed the book and are interested on further updates or just a place to share your thoughts with other readers or myself, please join my Facebook group by scanning below!

If you would be interested on receiving a FREE Planner for kids PDF version, by signing up you will also receive exclusive notifications to when new content is released and will be able to receive it at a promotional price. Scan below to sign up!

Scan below to check out my content on You Tube and learn more about Neurodiversity!

References

Abraham, K., & Studaker, M. (n.d.). *Intimidating teen behavior: Is it ODD or conduct disorder?*. Empowering Parents. https://www.empoweringparents.com/article/intimidating-teen-behavior-is-it-odd-or-conduct-disorder/

Adolescent development. (2023, May 1). Cleveland Clinic. https://my.clevelandclinic.org/health/articles/7060-adolescent-development

Allen, S. A. (n.d.). Sarah Addison Allen quote. Goodreads. https://www.goodreads.com/author/show/566874.Sarah_Addison_Allen

Arky, B. (2016, February 2). *Going to college with autism.* Child Mind Institute. https://childmind.org/article/going-to-college-with-autism/

Athar, K. (2023, August 6). *10 habits of highly independent people (and how you can cultivate them too).* Hack Spirit. https://hackspirit.com/habits-independent-people/

Avoiding social interaction: The dilemma for teens on the autism spectrum. (2017, April). My ASD Child. https://www.myaspergerschild.com/2017/04/avoiding-social-interaction-dilemma-for.html?m=1

Bédard, R. (2020, July 27). *Am I overparenting my child on the autism spectrum?*. Autism Parenting Magazine.

https://www.autismparentingmagazine.com/overparen ting-with-autism/

Beins, K. (2021, August 5). *Q&A expert advice on how to manage ASD behavior without yelling.* Autism Parenting Magazine. https://www.autismparentingmagazine.com/managing-asd-behavior-without-yelling/

Boys & Girls Clubs of America. (2023). *Youth right now.* https://www.bgca.org/about-us/youth-right-now

Boys & Girls Clubs of America. (2022, June 17). *Ways to build trust between parents and teens.* https://www.bgca.org/news-stories/2022/June/ways-to-build-trust-between-parents-and-teens

Burkeman, O. (2015, November 20). *Why you only need five things on your to-do list.* The Guardian. https://www.theguardian.com/lifeandstyle/2015/nov/20/oliver-burkeman-time-to-ditch-to-do-list

Challenging behaviour: autistic children and teenagers. (2020, November 18). Raising Children Network. https://raisingchildren.net.au/autism/behaviour/under standing-behaviour/challenging-behaviour-asd

Defiance in teens. (n.d.). Idaho Youth Ranch. https://www.youthranch.org/defiance

Depression and low mood: Autistic teenagers. (2023, April 17). Raising Children Network. https://raisingchildren.net.au/autism/health-wellbeing/mental-health/depression-teens-with-asd

Dubin, A. (2021, June 2). *Power struggles with kids, explained.* Moshi. https://www.moshikids.com/articles/power-struggles-kids/

Editors of Encyclopædia Britannica. (2023, August 14). *Special relativity.* Britannica. https://www.britannica.com/science/special-relativity

8 Practical college alternatives. (2021, March 11). OnPoint. https://www.onpointcu.com/blog/8-practical-college-alternatives/

Einstein was a "troubled teen." (2015, July 6). Eagle Ranch Academy. https://eagleranchacademy.com/einstein-was-a-troubled-teen/

Firestone, L. (2016, April 12). *What to do when your teen pushes you away.* PsychAlive. https://www.psychalive.org/what-to-do-when-teen-pushes-away/#:~:text=No%20matter%20how%20great%20a

French, M. (2021, October 5). *6 Teachable moments every parent should recognize.* BabyQuip. https://www.babyquip.com/blog/teachable-moments

Galarita, B. (2023, March 7). *What is an apprenticeship program? Here's what you should know.* Forbes. https://www.forbes.com/advisor/education/what-is-an-apprenticeship/

Garnett, M., & Attwood, T. (2022, May 5). *10 Challenges your autistic teenager likely faces every day.* Attwood & Garnett Events. https://attwoodandgarnettevents.com/10-challenges-your-autistic-teenager-likely-faces-every-day/

Gilmore, H. (2019, August 31). *11 Social skills for teens with ASD.* Psych Central. https://psychcentral.com/pro/child-therapist/2019/08/11-social-skills-for-teens-with-asd#1

Gongala, S. (2023, July 12). *Understanding teenage behavior problems and tips to handle them.* MomJunction. https://www.momjunction.com/articles/important-teenage-behavioural-problems-solutions_0010084/

Gregory, A. A. (2022, November 4). *35 Scripts for trauma survivors to set family boundaries.* PsychologyToday. https://www.psychologytoday.com/intl/blog/simplifyi ng-complex-trauma/202211/35-scripts-trauma-survivors-set-family-boundaries

Harrison, T. (n.d.). Thea Harrison quote. Goodreads. https://www.goodreads.com/author/show/4443809.T hea_Harrison

Helping kids identify and express feelings. (2018, January 6). Kids Helpline. https://kidshelpline.com.au/parents/issues/helping-kids-identify-and-express-feelings

Hendrickx, S. (2018, June 19). *Anxiety and autism in the classroom.* National Autistic Society. https://www.autism.org.uk/advice-and-guidance/professional-practice/anxiety-classroom

Henry Ford Health Staff. (2021, March 25). *Why children need positive reinforcement.* Henry Ford Health. https://www.henryford.com/blog/2021/03/positive-

reinforcement#:~:text=How%20does%20positive%20
reinforcement%20help

How to discipline a child on the autism spectrum. (2021, March 9). Therapeutic Pathways. https://www.tpathways.org/faqs/how-to-discipline-a-child-on-the-autism-spectrum/

How to make a vision board. (2020, June 19). Teen Breathe. https://teenbreathe.com.au/activities/how-to-make-a-vision-board/

How to reduce school anxiety in children on the spectrum. (2011, September). My ASD Child. https://www.myaspergerschild.com/2011/09/how-to-reduce-school-anxiety-in.html?m=1

Hudson, A. (2023, July 15). *13 ways on how to help your teen make friends.* Ashley Hudson Therapy. https://www.ashleyhudsontherapy.com/post/13-ways-on-how-to-help-your-teen-make-friends

Indeed Editorial Team. (2023, February 3). *15 Visualization techniques to help you achieve your goals.* Indeed. https://www.indeed.com/career-advice/career-development/visualization-techniques

Indeed Editorial Team. (2023, March 16). *10 ways to start a conversation (plus 15 ice breakers).* Indeed Career Guide. https://www.indeed.com/career-advice/career-development/how-to-start-a-conversation

Jenn. (2022, May 31). *20 of the best inspirational quotes for kids.* Comeback Momma.

https://www.comebackmomma.com/best-
inspirational-quotes-for-kids/

Kimmel, T. (n.d.). *Teenage rebellion quotes* (7 quotes). Goodreads.
https://www.goodreads.com/quotes/tag/teenage-
rebellion#:~:text=If%20your%20life%20is%20a

Körner, R., & Schütz, A. (2021). Power in romantic
relationships: How positional and experienced power
are associated with relationship quality. *Journal of Social
and Personal Relationships, 38*(9), 2653-2677.
https://doi.org/10.1177/02654075211017670

Lehman, J. (n.d.). *Avoid power struggles with children*. Empowering
Parents.
https://www.empoweringparents.com/article/avoiding
-power-struggles-defiant-children-declaring-victory-
easier-think/

Lehman, J. (2019). *Does your child have toxic friends? How to deal
with the wrong crowd.* Empowering Parents.
https://www.empoweringparents.com/article/does-
your-child-have-toxic-friends-6-ways-to-deal-with-the-
wrong-crowd/

Lewis, R. (2023, February 8). *Erikson's 8 stages of psychosocial
development, explained for parents.* Healthline.
https://www.healthline.com/health/parenting/erikson
-stages

Linnell-Olsen, L. (2022, June 13). *How do kids spend the school
day? Recommended times and structure.* Verywell Family.
https://www.verywellfamily.com/time-needs-for-
youth-activities-4083024

Lowell, E. (n.d.). Elizabeth Lowell quote. Goodreads. https://www.goodreads.com/author/show/19051.Elizabeth_Lowell

Lucas, R. (2017, December 21). *5 super successful people who don't have a degree.* News24. https://www.news24.com/you/celebs/5-super-successful-people-who-dont-have-a-degree-20171220

M, K. (2023, July 13). *121 best and inspirational parenting quotes of all time.* MomJunction. https://www.momjunction.com/articles/amazing-quotes-on-parenting-to-inspire-you_00104303/

Maïano, C., Normand, C. L., Salvas, M.-C., Moullec, G., & Aimé, A. (2015). Prevalence of school bullying among youth with autism spectrum disorders: A systematic review and meta-analysis. *Autism Research, 9*(6), 601–615. https://doi.org/10.1002/aur.1568

Masterclass. (2022, November 9). *Leading from behind: How to lead from behind.* Masterclass. https://www.masterclass.com/articles/leading-from-behind

Meltzer, M. (2015, July 13). *10 simple calm down strategies for teens.* North Shore Pediatric Therapy. https://www.nspt4kids.com/parenting/10-simple-calm-down-strategies-for-teens/

Miller, C. (2017, July 18). *7 reasons threats don't work and what to do instead.* Keeping Your Cool Parenting. https://keepingyourcoolparenting.com/stop-with-the-threats-7-reasons-threats-dont-work-and-what-to-do-instead/

Mind Tools Content Team. (n.d.). *Role-playing*. MindTools. https://www.mindtools.com/acjtx9g/role-playing

Morin, A. (2021, February 12). *7 life skills your teen needs to be independent*. Verywell Family. https://www.verywellfamily.com/life-skills-your-teen-needs-to-be-independent-2609033

Morin, A. (2022, November 2). *23 inspiring parenting quotes to help you stay motivated*. Verywell Family. https://www.verywellfamily.com/inspirational-parenting-quotes-1094736

Moss, H. (2021, April 6). *30 quotes from 30 people with autism*. Els for Autism. https://www.elsforautism.org/30-quotes-from-30-people-with-autism/

MumzWorld. (2017, August 21). *How to win an argument against your parents*. Mumzworld. https://blog.mumzworld.com/how-to-win-an-argument-against-your-parents/

National Autistic Society. (2022). *Dealing with bullying - a guide for parents and carers*. https://autism.org.uk/advice-and-guidance/topics/bullying/bullying/parents

Nelson, R. (2015, April 2). *Determining if your teen's acting out is normal behavior*. ViewPoint Center. https://www.viewpointcenter.com/determining-teens-acting-out-is-normal-behavior/

Oppositional defiant disorder (ODD). (2021, May 12). PsychDB. https://www.psychdb.com/child/disruptive-impulsive/odd

Oppositional defiant disorder vs. normal teenage rebellion. (2019, July 5). Turn-About Ranch. https://www.turnaboutranch.com/2019/07/ODD-vs-normal-teen-rebellion/#:~:text=It%20may%20be%20considered%20normal

Over-parenting kids on the autism spectrum. (2019, March 24). Life with Aspergers. https://life-with-aspergers.blogspot.com/2019/03/aspergers-and-over-parenting.html?m=1

Raser, J. (n.d.). *Power struggles quotes* (6 quotes). Goodreads. https://www.goodreads.com/quotes/tag/power-struggles

Rudy, L. J. (2022, June 1). *Why school is so challenging for children with autism.* Verywell Health. https://www.verywellhealth.com/why-school-is-so-challenging-4000048

Ryan, N. (2021, August 19). *What to do when your teen is starting to pull away.* Relationship Therapy Center. https://www.therelationshiptherapycenter.com/blog/2021/8/12/what-to-do-when-your-teen-is-starting-to-pull-away

Shutterfly Community. (2023, August 3). *55+ Inspirational school quotes for every student.* Shutterfly. https://www.shutterfly.com/ideas/school-quotes/

Silvera, A. (2020, February 10). *27 of the best YA book quotes about friendship*. BookRiot. https://bookriot.com/ya-book-quotes-about-friendship/

Social and emotional changes in pre-teens and teenagers. (2021, July 12). Raising Children Network. https://raisingchildren.net.au/pre-teens/development/social-emotional-development/social-emotional-changes-9-15-years

Stevenson, R. (2021, April 26). *Steve Jobs: The childhood of a great inventor*. BBC Science Focus Magazine. https://www.sciencefocus.com/future-technology/steve-jobs-the-childhood-of-a-great-inventor

Teens on the autism spectrum and low self-worth. (2019, June). My ASD Child. https://www.myaspergerschild.com/2019/06/teens-on-autism-spectrum-and-low-self.html?m=1

10 ways to help your kids stand up to peer pressure. (2010, August 2). All pro Dad. https://www.allprodad.com/10-ways-to-help-kids-stand-up-to-peer-pressure/

TimesofIndia. (2020, March 23). *Warning signs that your child has a toxic friend and what can you do to help*. The Times of India. https://timesofindia.indiatimes.com/life-style/parenting/teen/warning-signs-that-your-child-has-a-toxic-friend-and-what-can-you-do-to-help/articleshow/74748278.cms?from=mdr

Uche, U. (2017, July 3). *How to avoid power struggles with your teen*. Psychology Today.

https://www.psychologytoday.com/za/blog/promotin
g-empathy-your-teen/201707/how-avoid-power-
struggles-your-teen

University of Wisconsin-Madison. (2022, May 4). *UW study: Most teens actually have healthy relationship with digital technology.* UW School of Medicine and Public Health. https://www.med.wisc.edu/news-and-events/2022/may/most-teens-have-good-relationship-with-technology/

Walker, B. (2023, April 3). *16 Millionaires who made their fortunes without a college degree.* FinanceBuzz. https://financebuzz.com/millionaires-without-a-college-degree

Wambui, F. (2020, August 21). *Parenting: 8 ways to mentor your kids at home.* Potentash Africa. https://potentash.com/2020/08/21/ways-mentor-kids-home-parenting/

Wendt, T. (2022, August 25). *What to know about autism spectrum disorder in teens.* WebMD. https://www.webmd.com/brain/autism/what-to-know-about-autism-spectrum-disorder-teens

Why "traditional discipline" doesn't work for many kids on the autism spectrum. (2018, December). My ASD Child. https://www.myaspergerschild.com/2018/12/why-traditional-discipline-doesnt-work.html?m=1

Willard, M. (2023, July 21). *Social skills issues in children.* Cadey. https://cadey.co/articles/social-skills

Willsey, M. (2021, February 12). *What did Albert Einstein invent?*. HowStuffWorks. https://science.howstuffworks.com/innovation/famous-inventors/what-did-albert-einstein-invent.htm

Young, K. (2015, June 3). *Teaching kids how to set and protect their boundaries against toxic behaviour.* Hey Sigmund. https://www.heysigmund.com/teaching-kids-how-to-set-boundaries-and-keep-toxic-people-out/comment-page-1/

Image References

Cameron, J. M. (2020). *A woman in green hoodie sitting near the table while having conversation through her desktop* [Image]. Pexels. https://www.pexels.com/photo/a-woman-in-green-hoodie-sitting-near-the-table-while-having-conversation-through-her-desktop-4144830/

Chung, Z. (2020). *Ethnic mother talking to daughter with gardening tools* [Image]. Pexels. https://www.pexels.com/photo/ethnic-mother-talking-to-daughter-with-gardening-tools-5529578/

Cottonbro Studio. (2020). *Young men and women in the library* [Image]. Pexels. https://www.pexels.com/photo/young-men-and-women-in-the-library-6214729/

Cottonbro Studio. (2021a). *A woman handing condoms to her daughter* [Image]. Pexels.

https://www.pexels.com/photo/a-woman-handing-condoms-to-her-daughter-6470998/

Cottonbro Studio. (2021b). *Fashion man love people* [Image]. Pexels. https://www.pexels.com/photo/fashion-man-love-people-6593908/

Fairytale, E. (2020). *Woman in white lace long sleeve shirt hugging another woman* [Image]. Pexels. https://www.pexels.com/photo/woman-in-white-lace-long-sleeve-shirt-hugging-another-woman-3893734/

Grabowska, K. (2021a). *Teenager fell asleep on wooden table top* [Image]. Pexels. https://www.pexels.com/photo/teenager-fell-asleep-on-wooden-table-top-6957113/

Grabowska, K. (2021b). *Woman showing to her daughter how to seat at a table during breakfast* [Image]. Pexels. https://www.pexels.com/photo/woman-showing-to-her-daughter-how-to-seat-at-a-table-during-breakfast-6957043/

Kampus Production. (2021). *Woman in white dress painting* [Image]. Pexels. https://www.pexels.com/photo/woman-in-white-dress-painting-8036845/

Kaysha. (2018). *A father and his teenage son posing on a balcony* [Image]. Pexels. https://www.pexels.com/photo/a-father-and-his-teenage-son-posing-on-a-balcony-960829/

Kindel Media. (2021a). *A mother and son inside a car* [Image]. Pexels. https://www.pexels.com/photo/a-mother-and-son-inside-a-car-8550826/

Kindel Media. (2021b). *Man scolding his son* [Image]. Pexels. https://www.pexels.com/photo/man-scolding-his-son-8550837/

Krukau, Y. (2021). *Woman in blue long sleeve shirt sitting beside man in red jacket* [Image]. Pexels. https://www.pexels.com/photo/woman-in-blue-long-sleeve-shirt-sitting-beside-man-in-red-jacket-8199568/

Kumtanom, T. (2017). *Man and woman sitting on bench in woods* [Image]. Pexels. https://www.pexels.com/photo/man-and-woman-sitting-on-bench-in-woods-450050/

Maidre, O. (2019). *Photo of man taking picture* [Image]. Pexels. https://www.pexels.com/photo/photo-of-man-taking-picture-2046773/

Milton, G. (2021). *Crop unrecognizable person applying glue on papers* [Image]. Pexels. https://www.pexels.com/photo/crop-unrecognizable-person-applying-glue-on-papers-7014490/

Pak, G. (2021). *Young man and woman walking together* [Image]. Pexels. https://www.pexels.com/photo/young-man-and-woman-walking-together-7973205/

Ranquist, E. (2018). *Photography of people graduating* [Image]. Pexels. https://www.pexels.com/photo/photography-of-people-graduating-1205651/

RDNE Stock Project. (2021). *Volunteers happily assisting an old man on a wheelchair for charity* [Image]. Pexels. https://www.pexels.com/photo/volunteers-happily-assisting-an-old-man-on-a-wheelchair-for-charity-6646916/

Rimoldi, A. (2020). *Multiracial students communicating and walking downstairs* [Image]. Pexels. https://www.pexels.com/photo/multiracial-students-communicating-and-walking-downstairs-5553021/